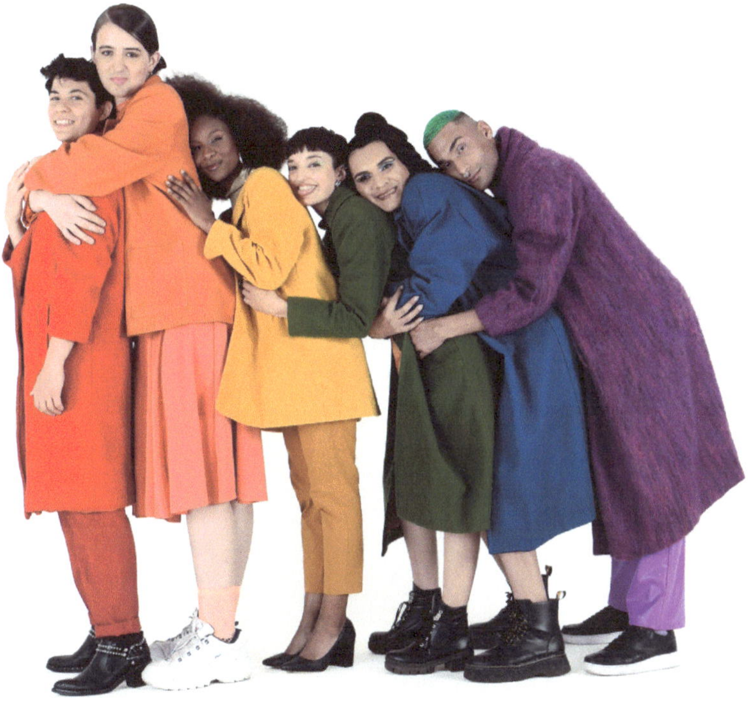

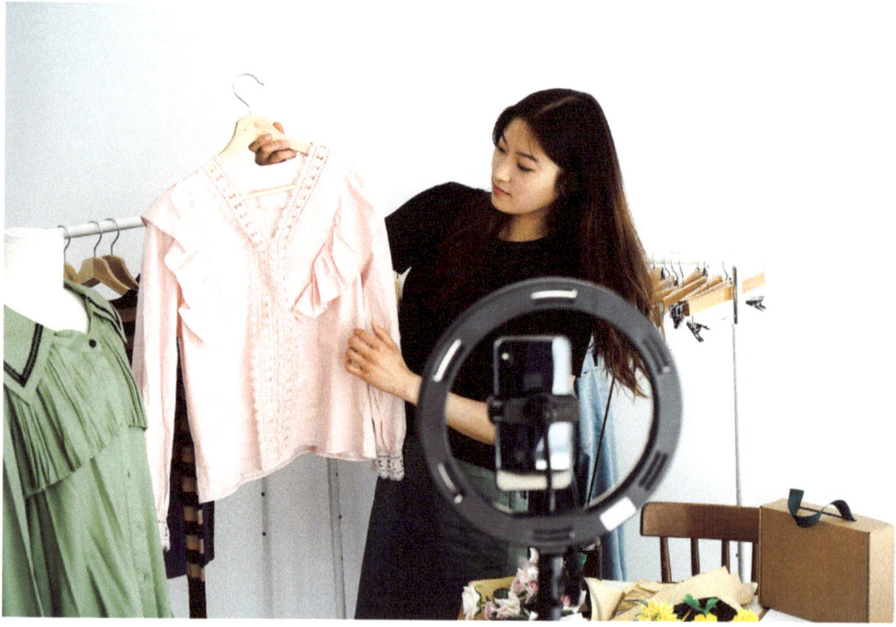

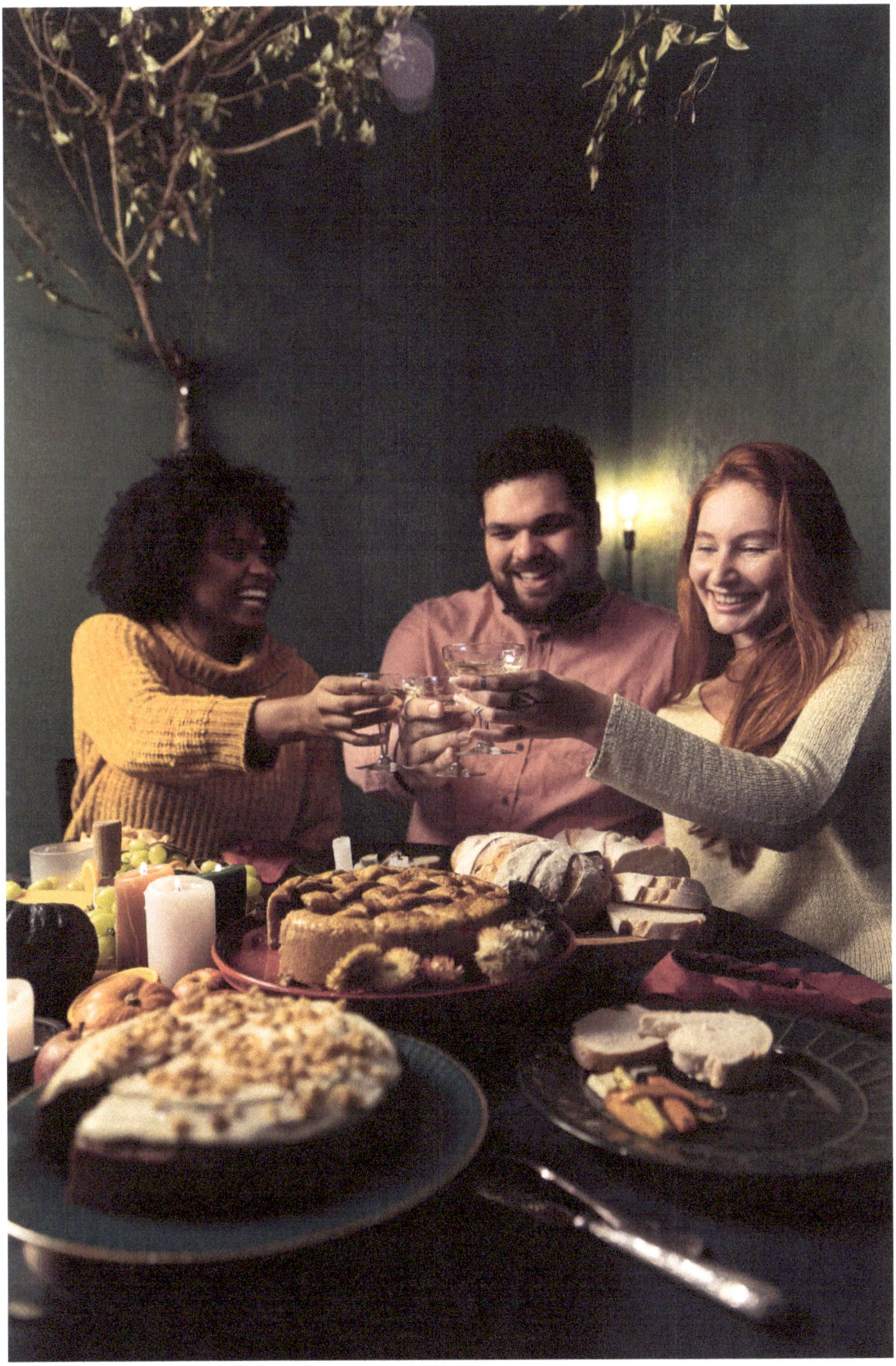

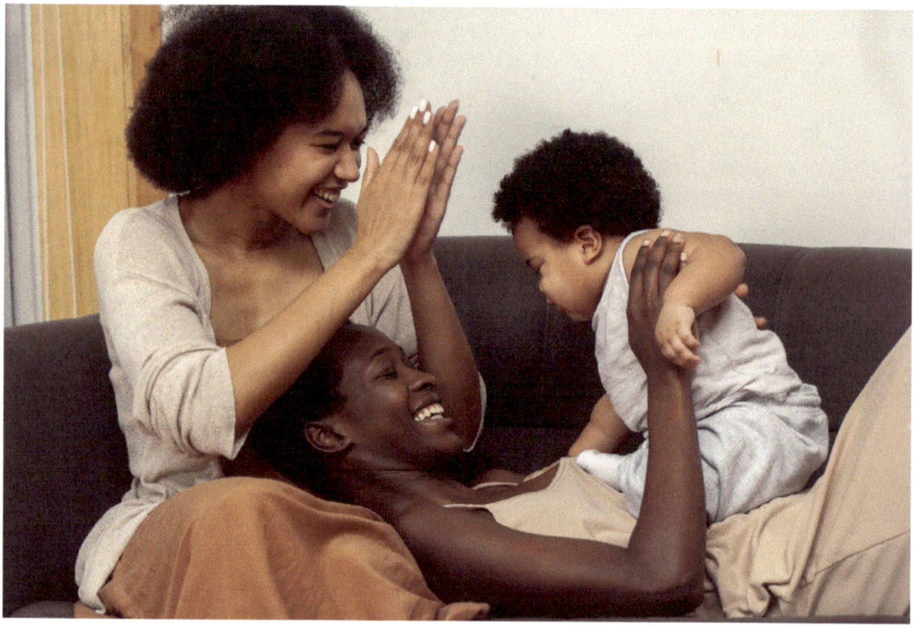

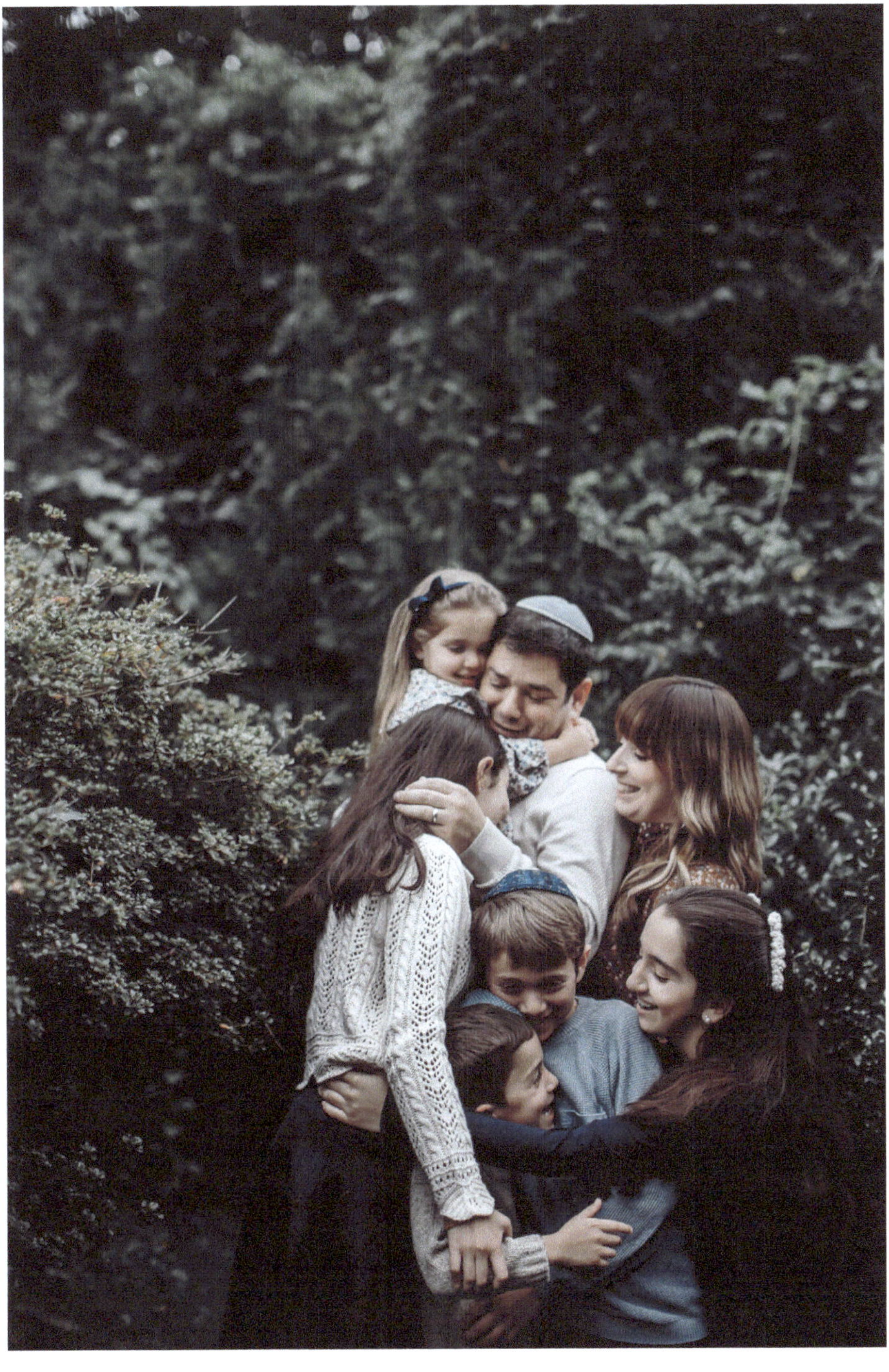

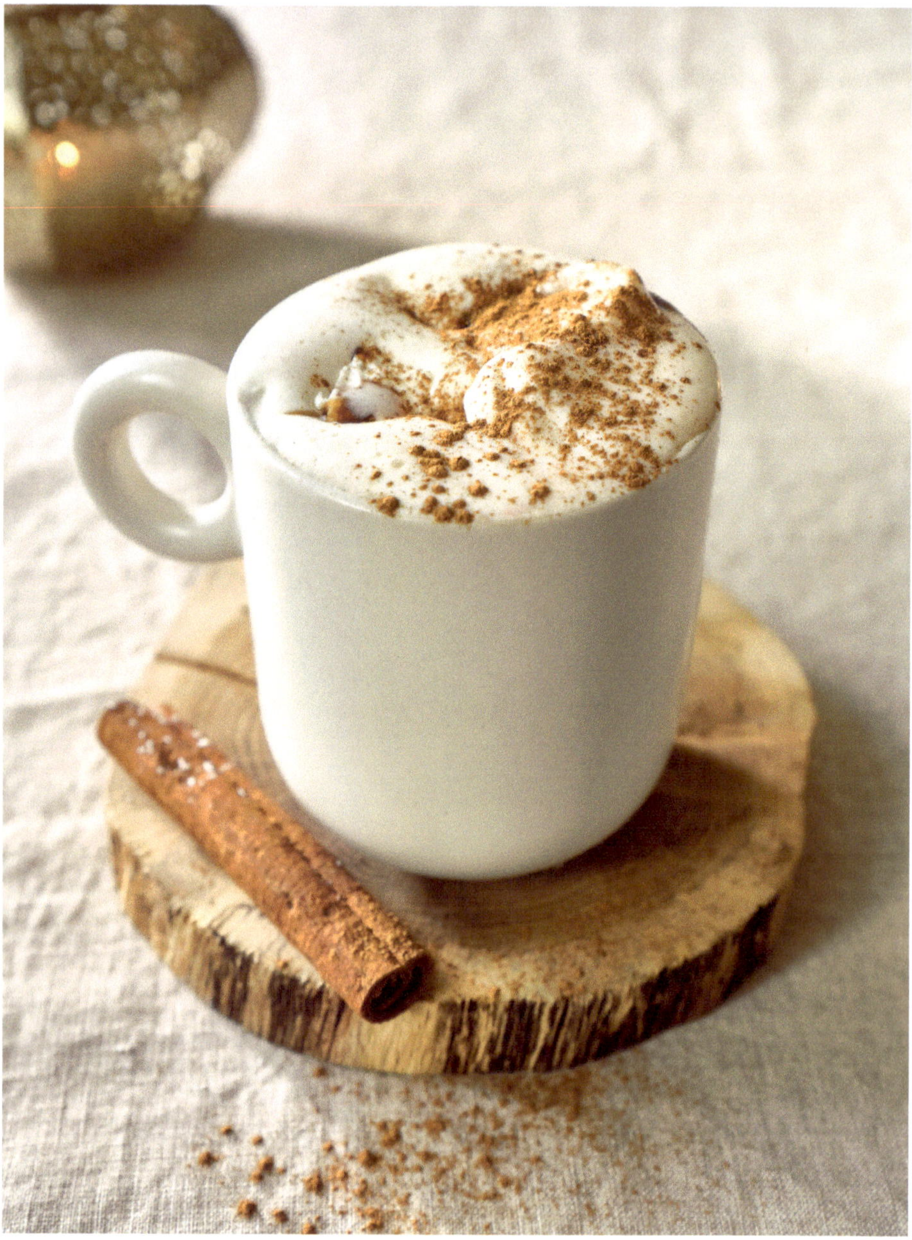

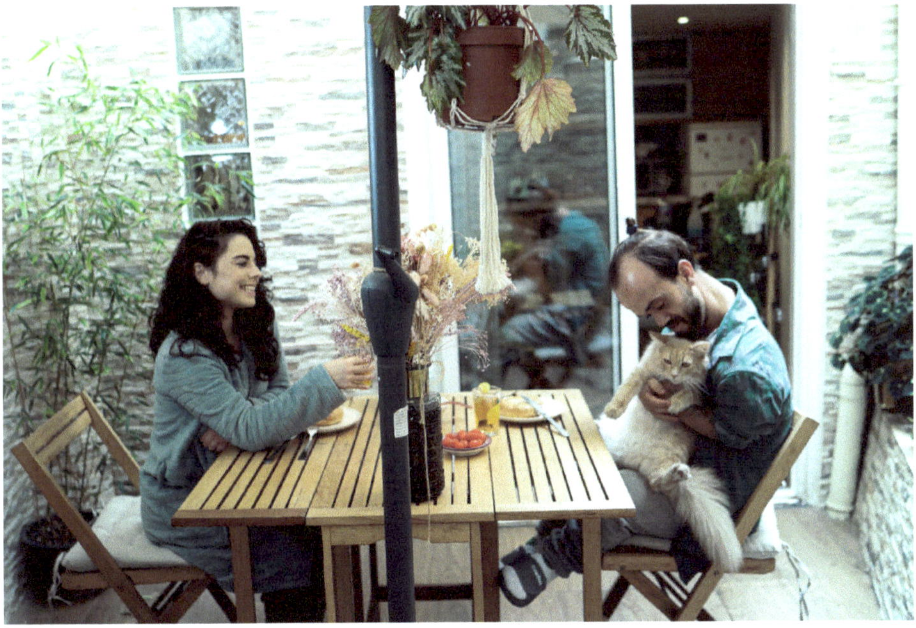

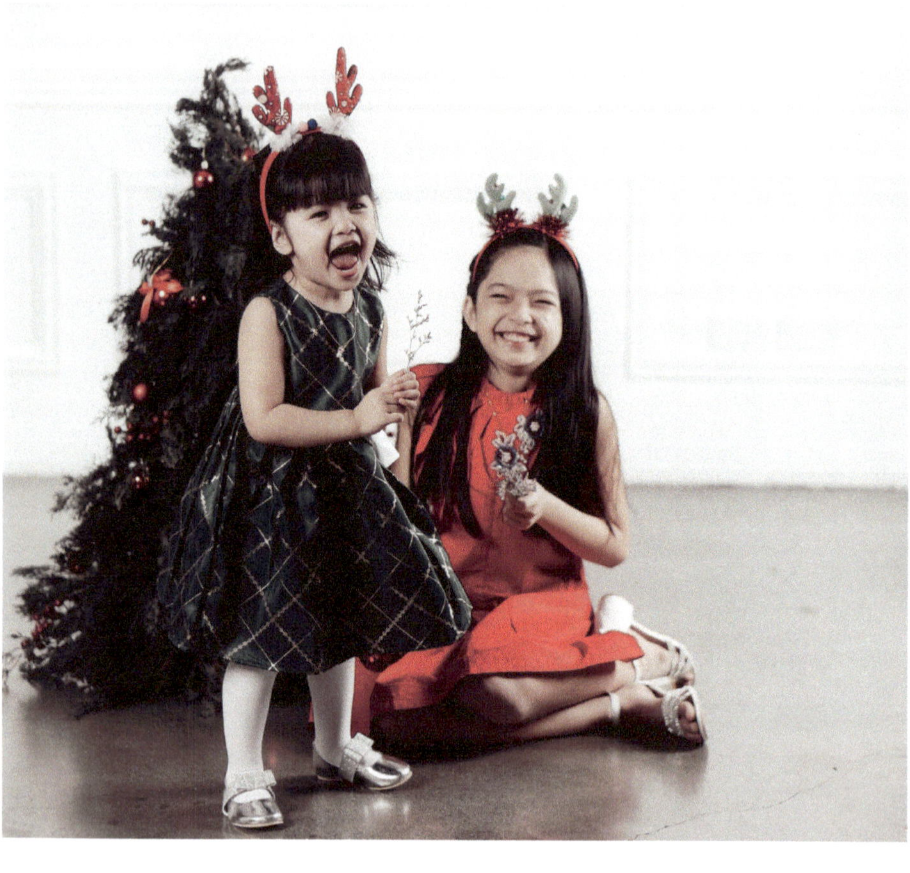

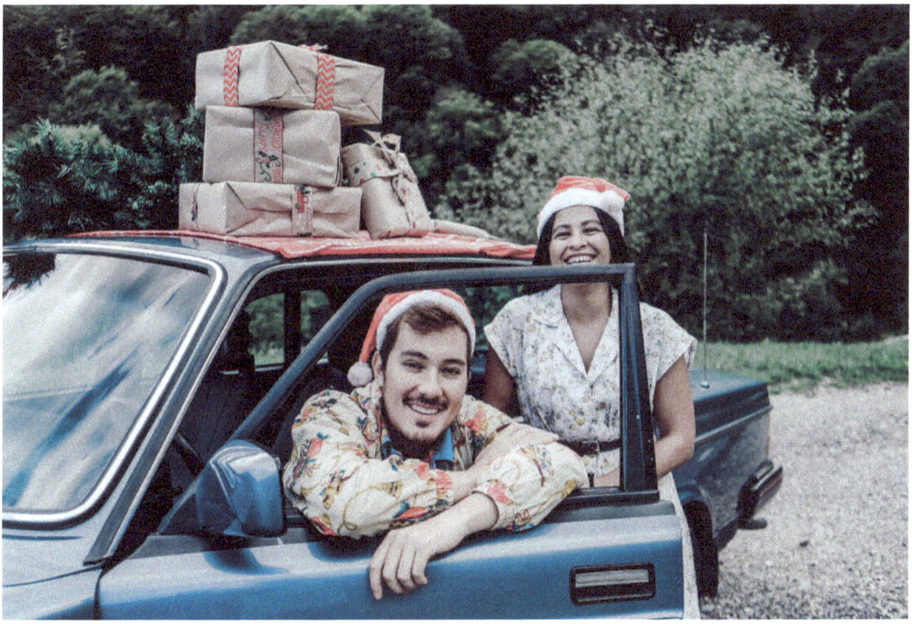

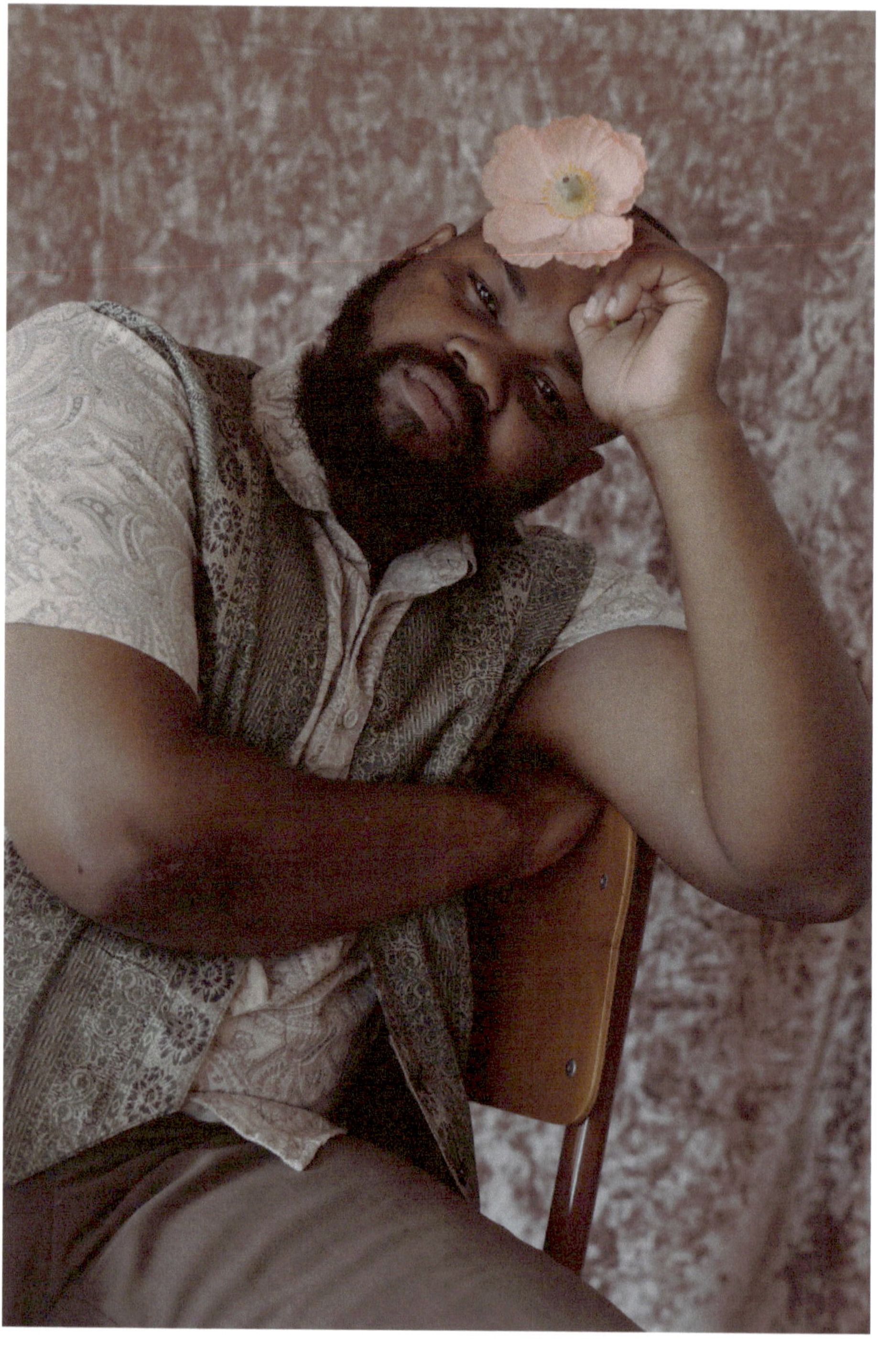

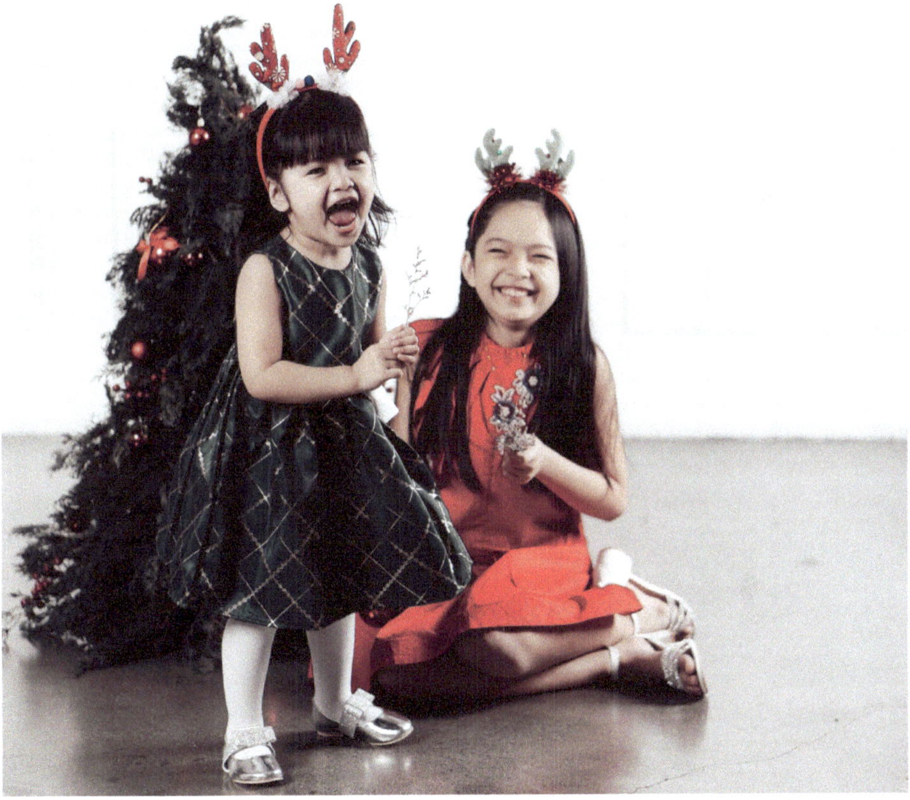

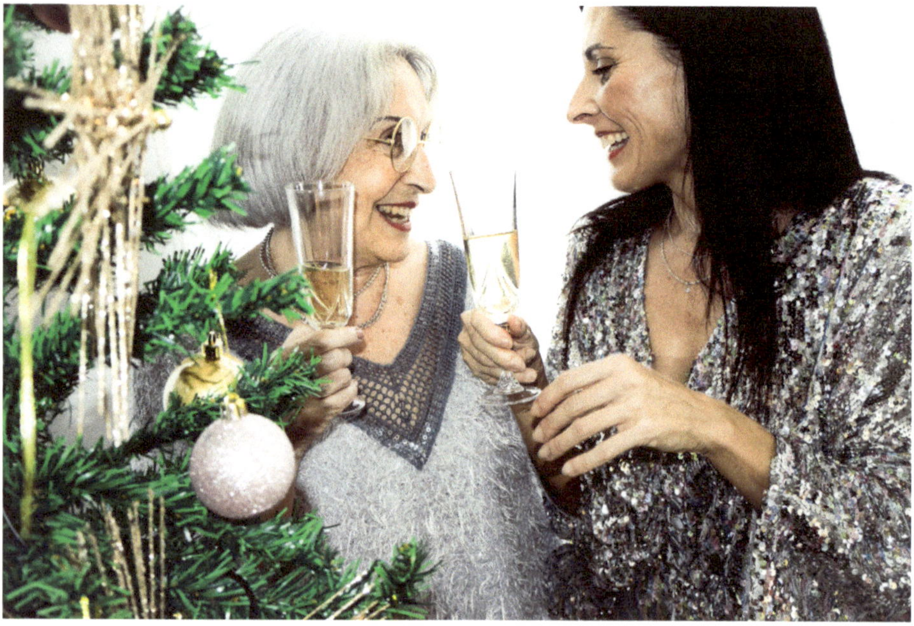

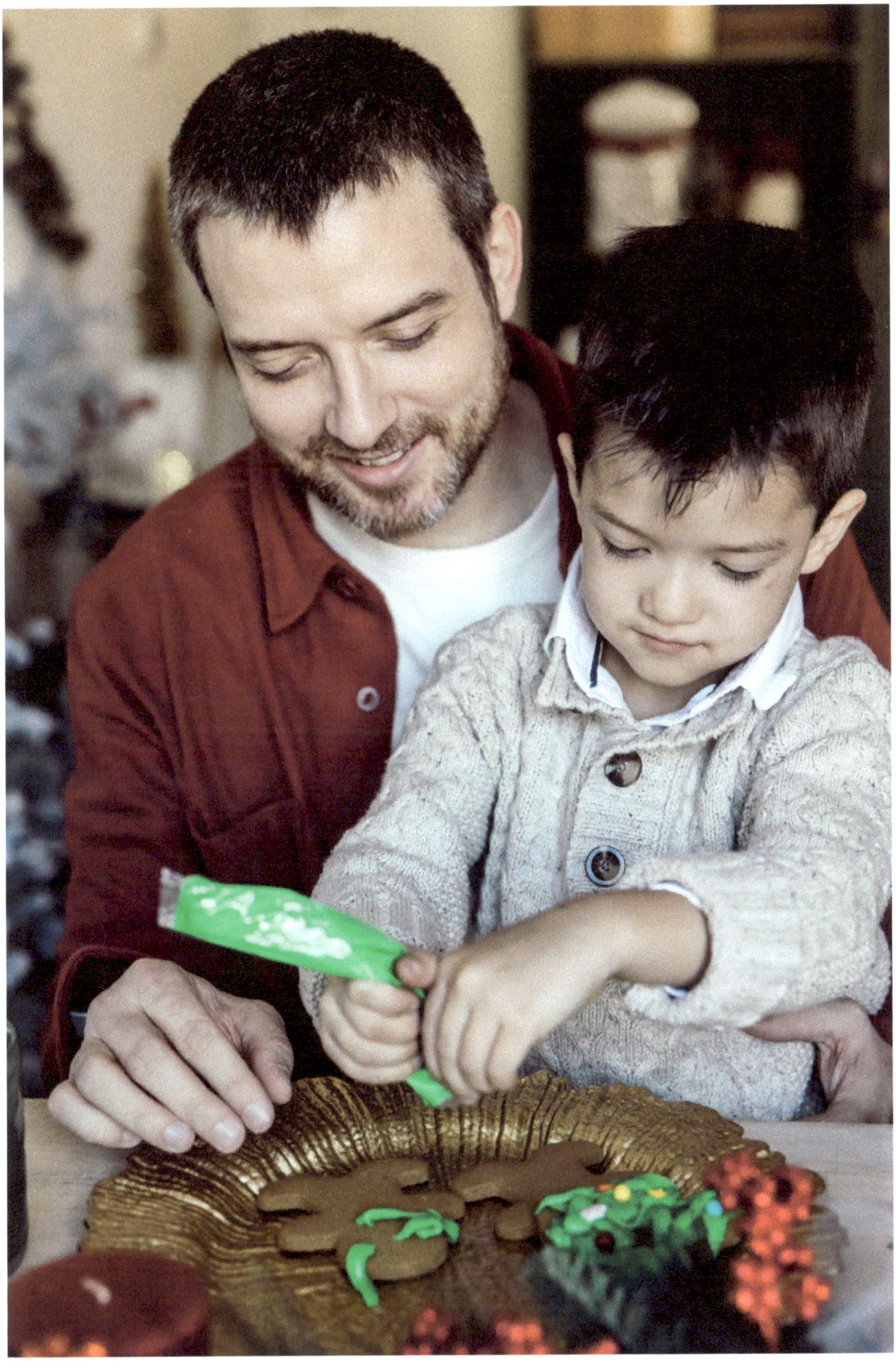

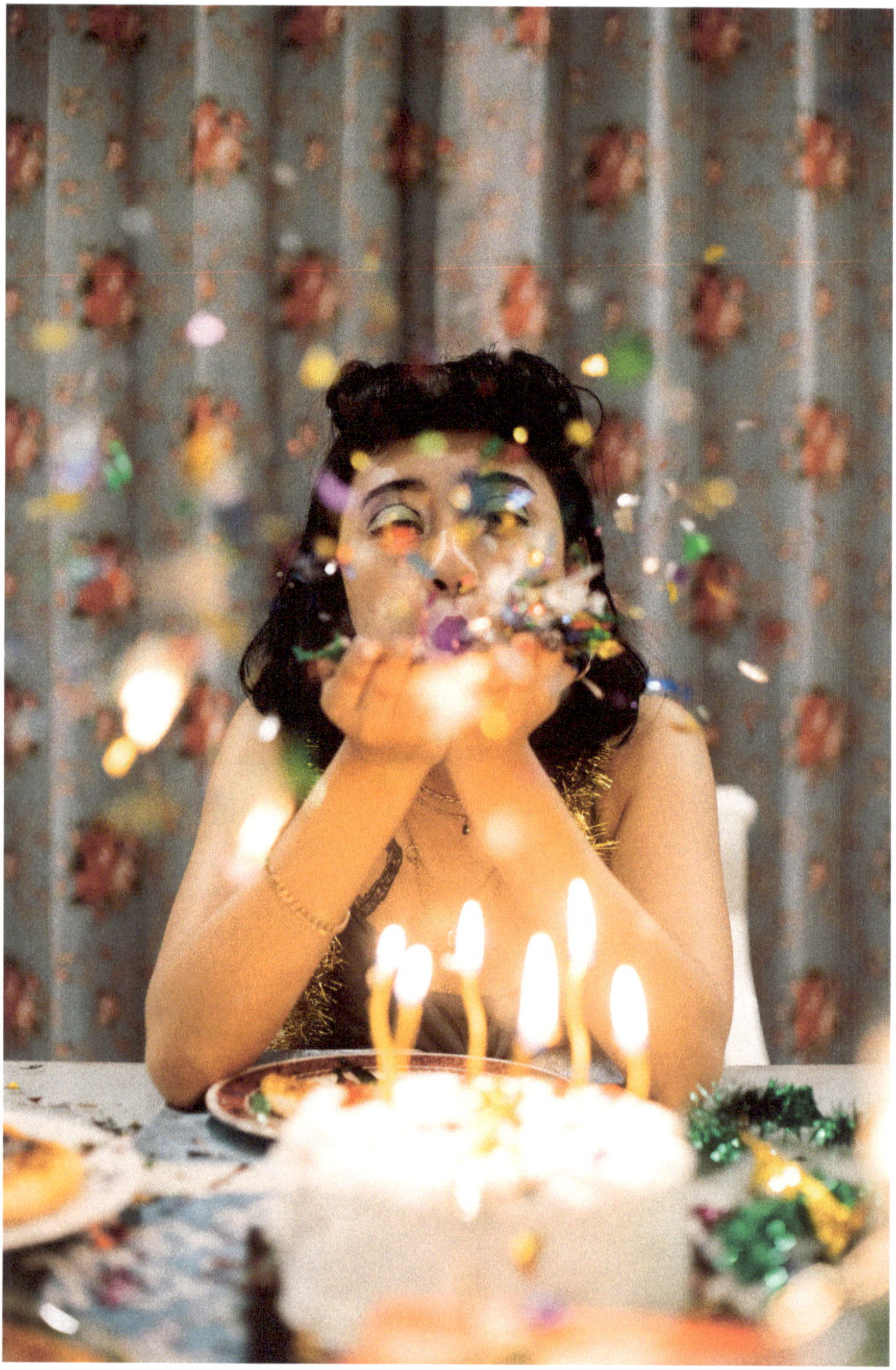

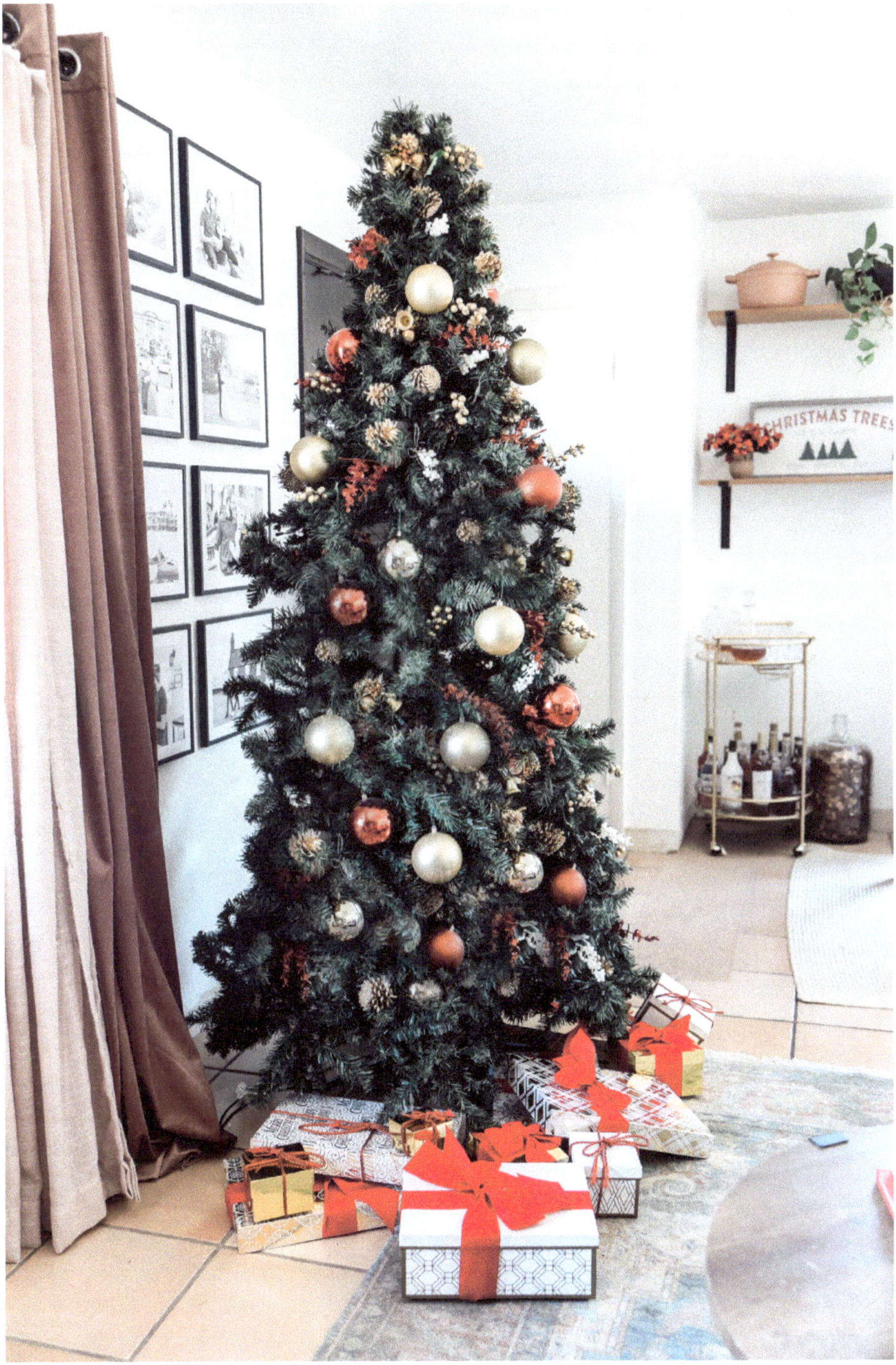
HRISTMAS TREES

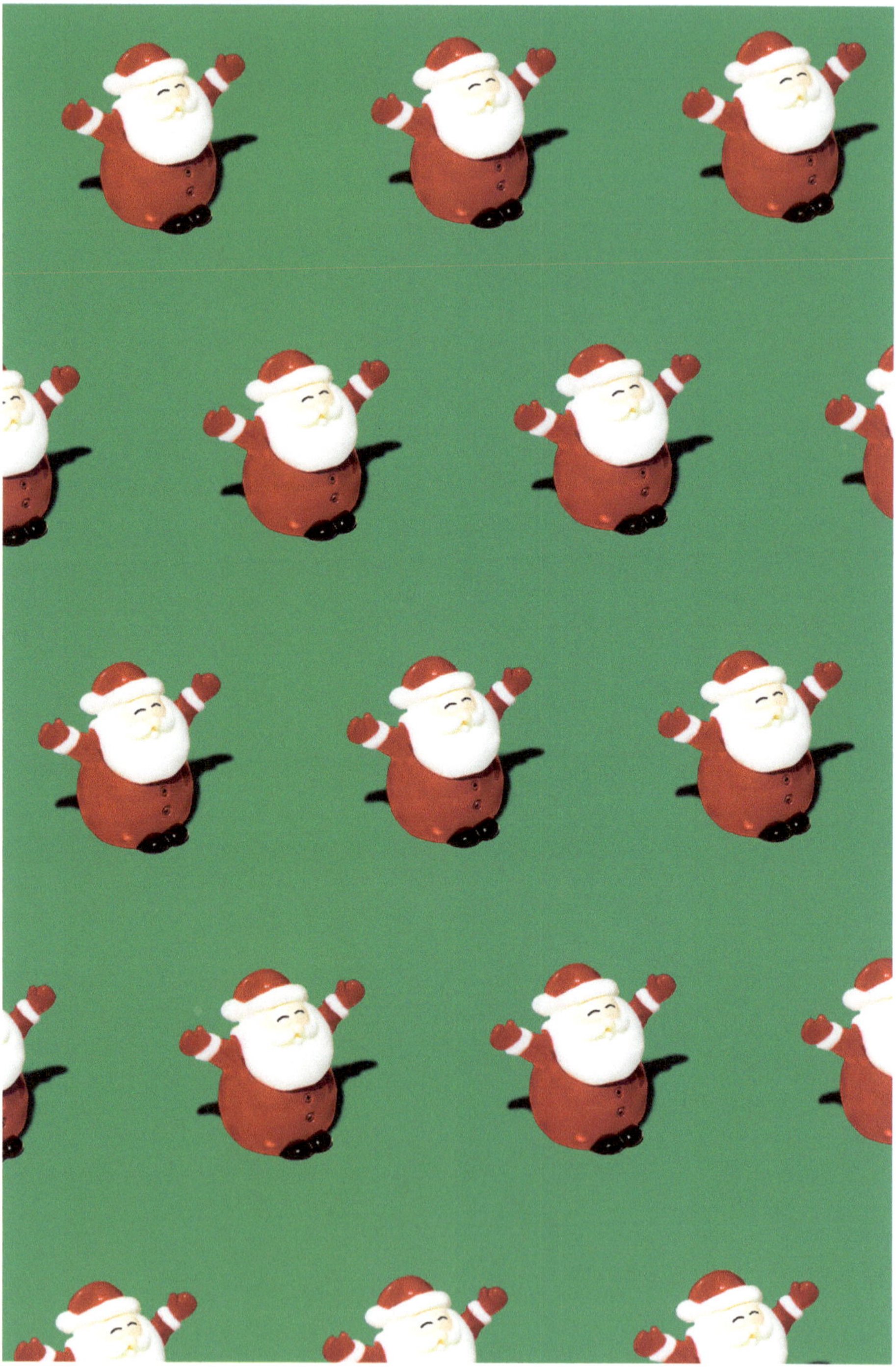

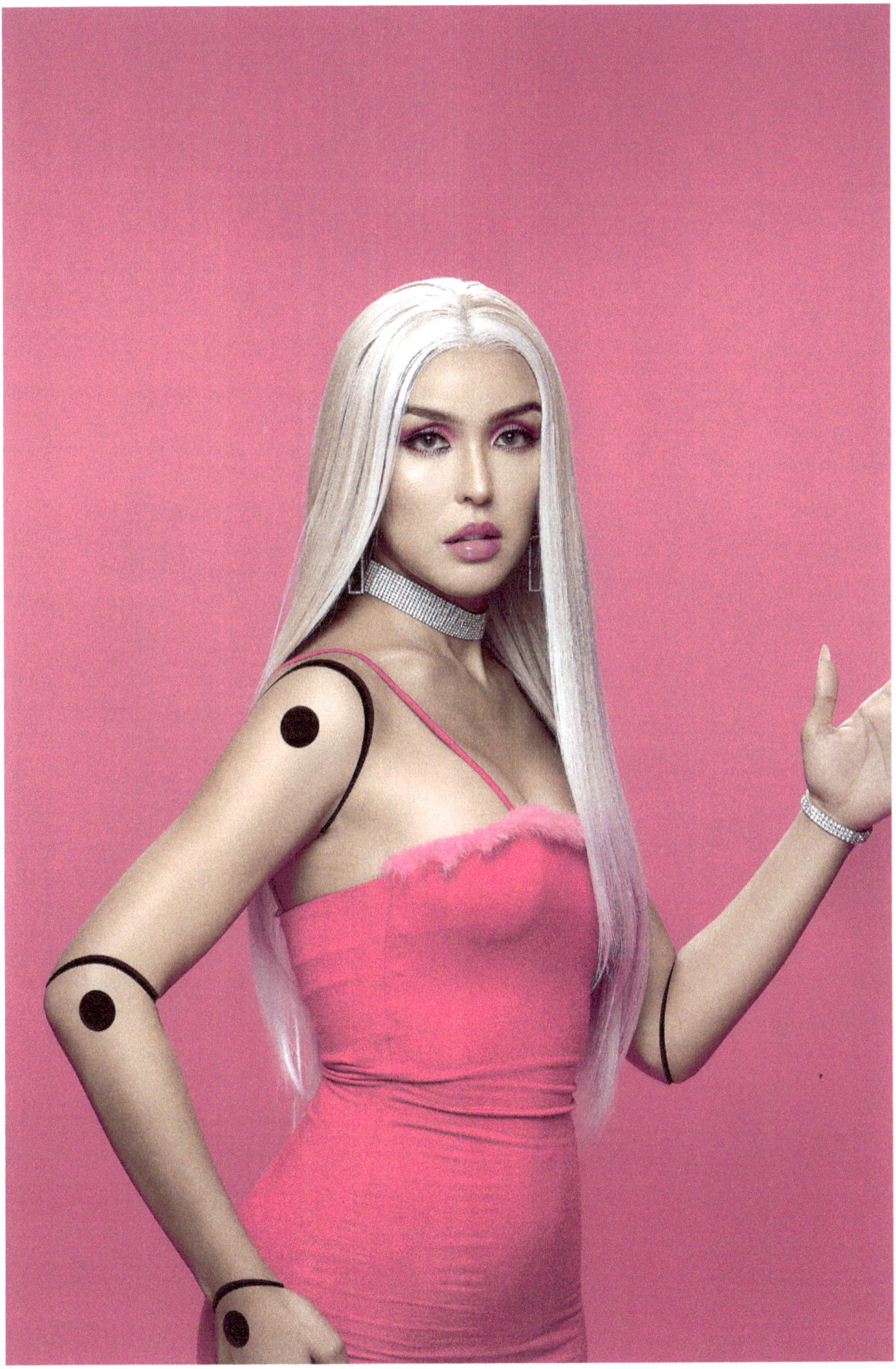

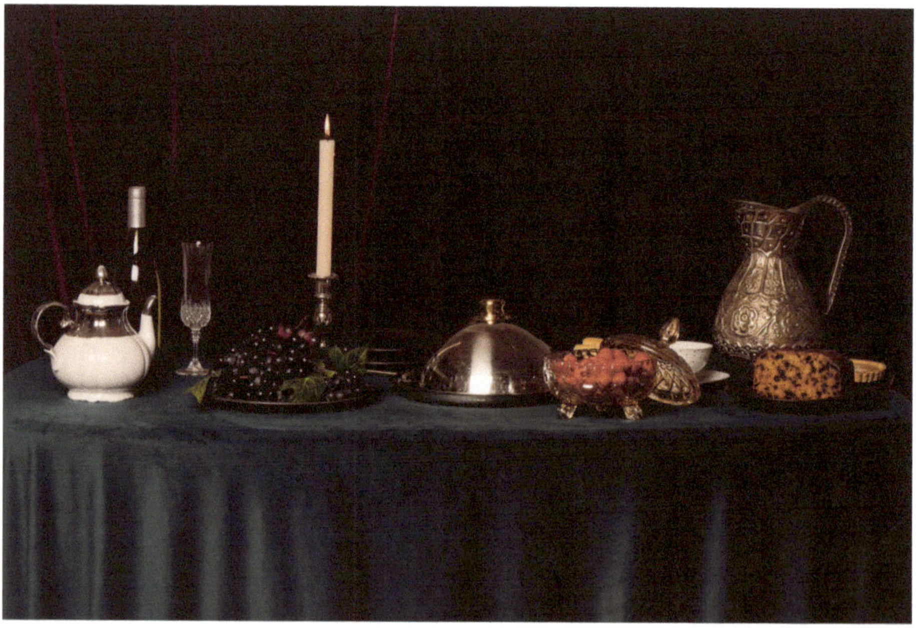

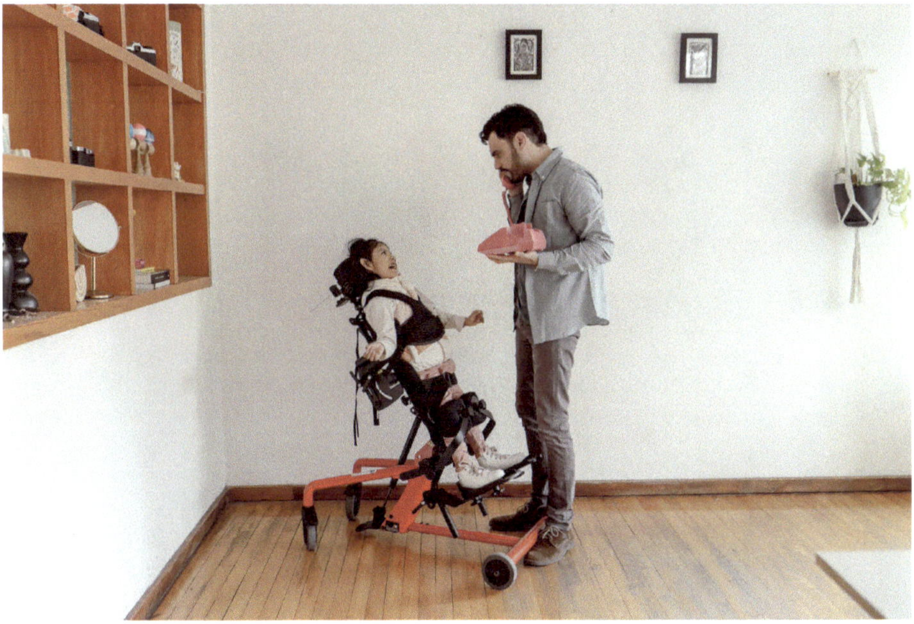

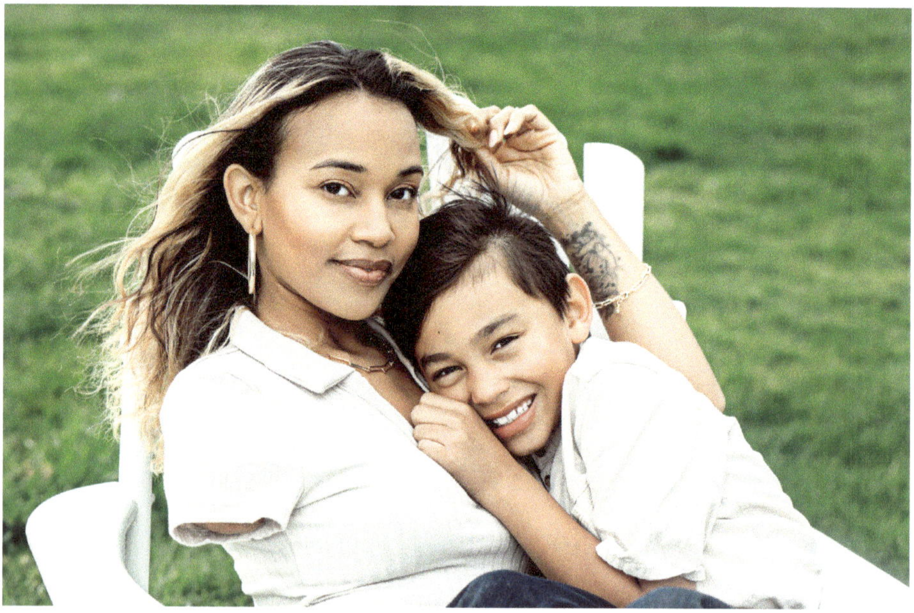

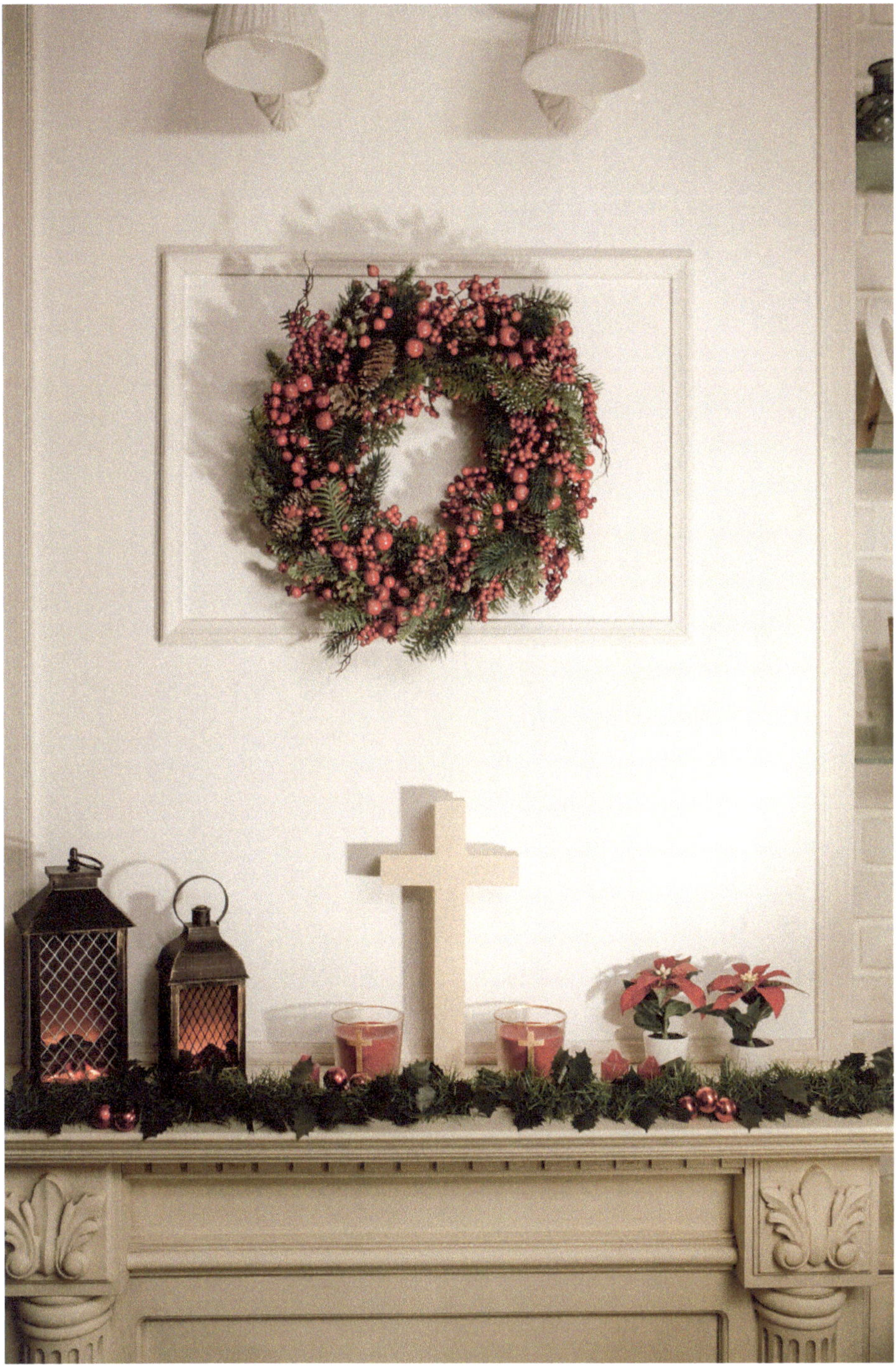

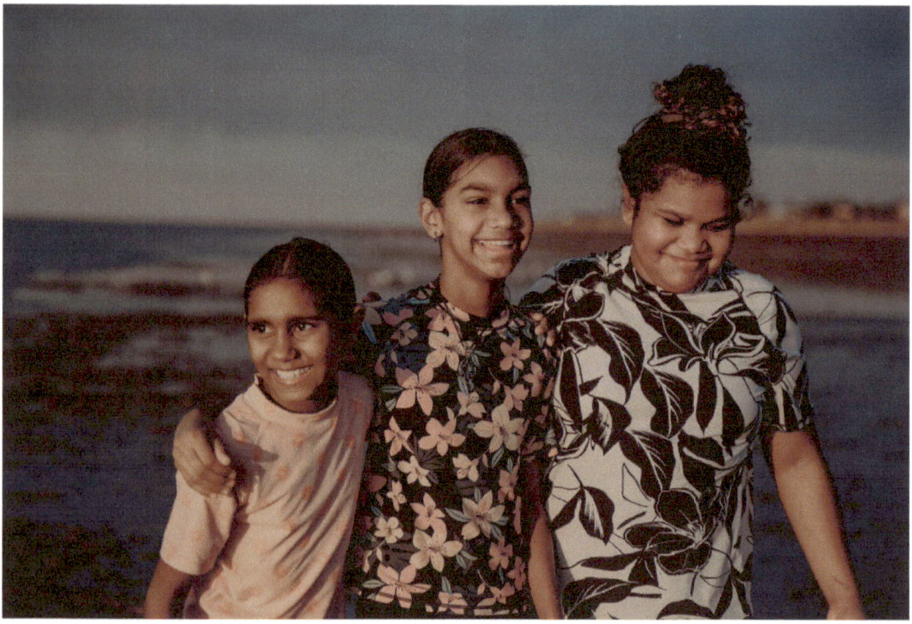

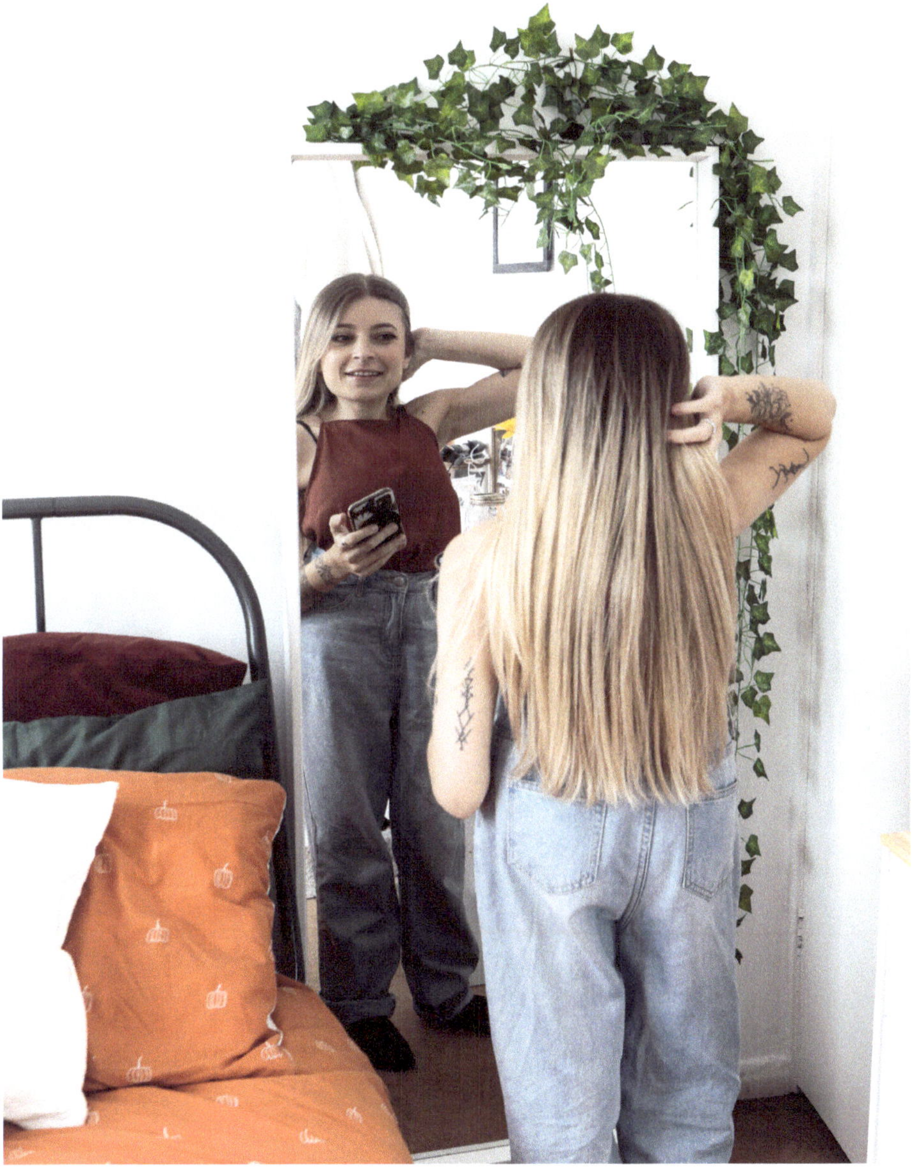

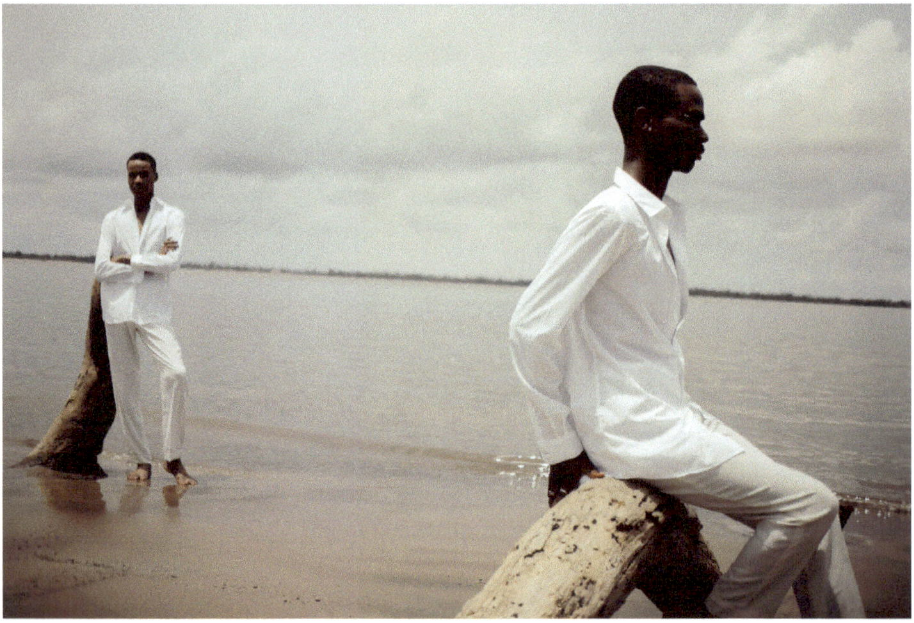

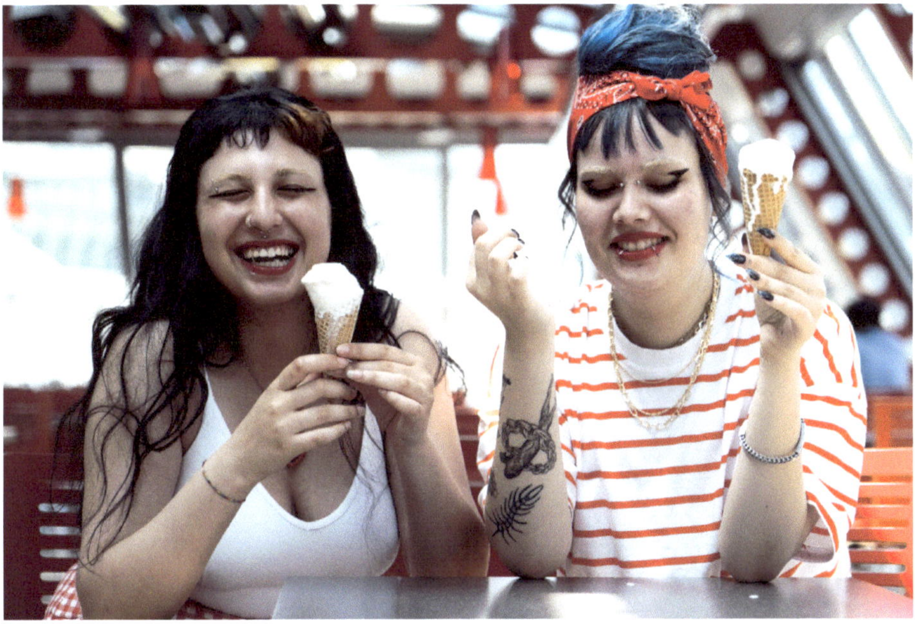

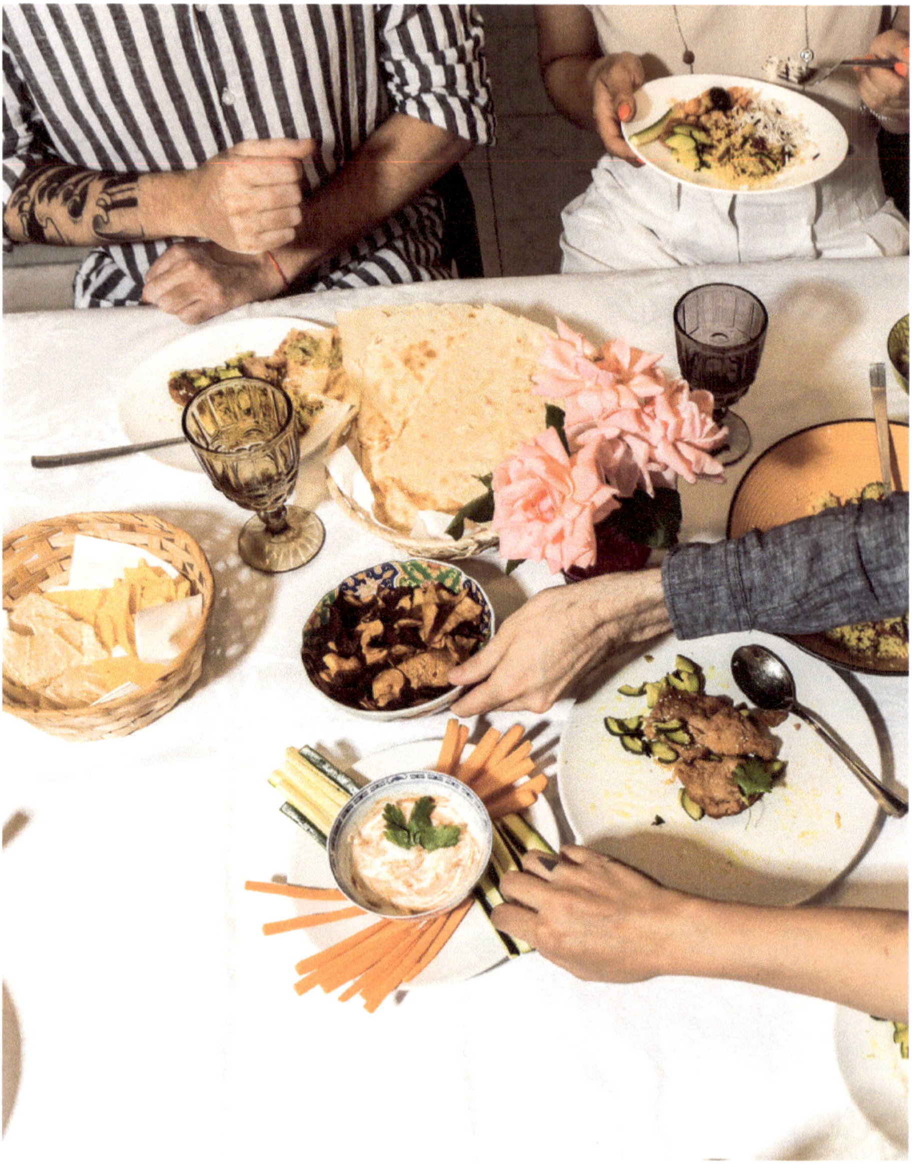

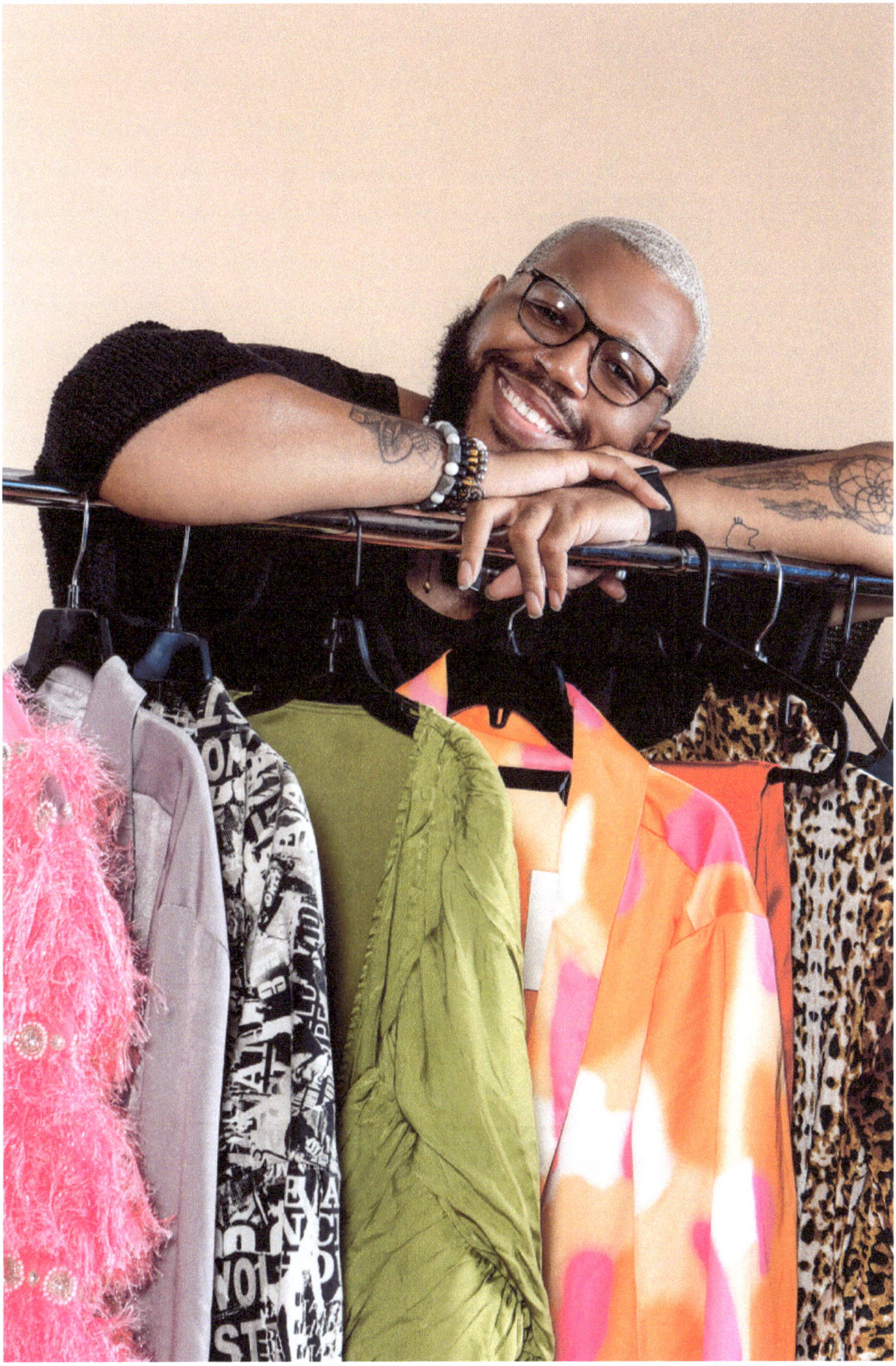

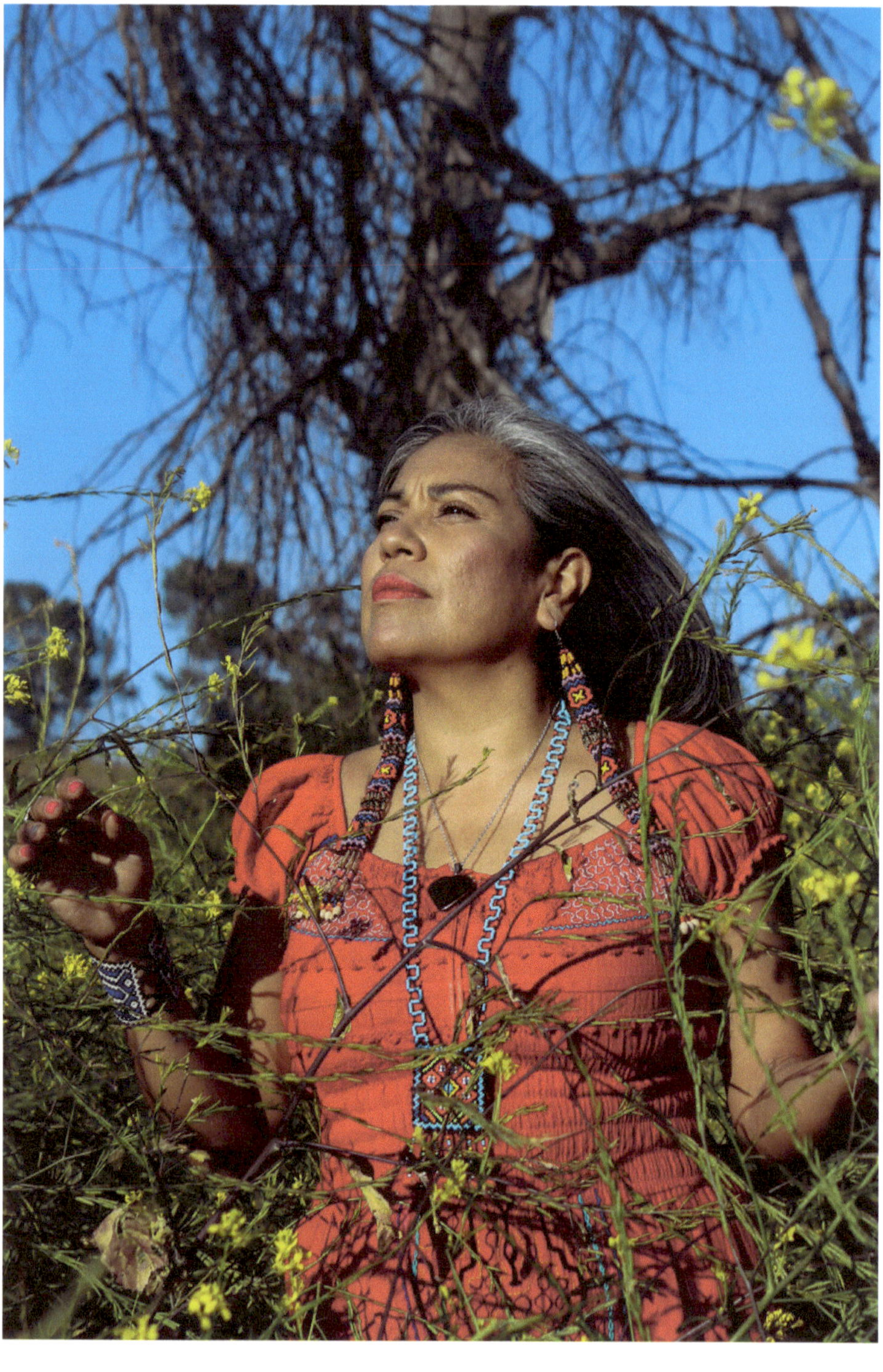

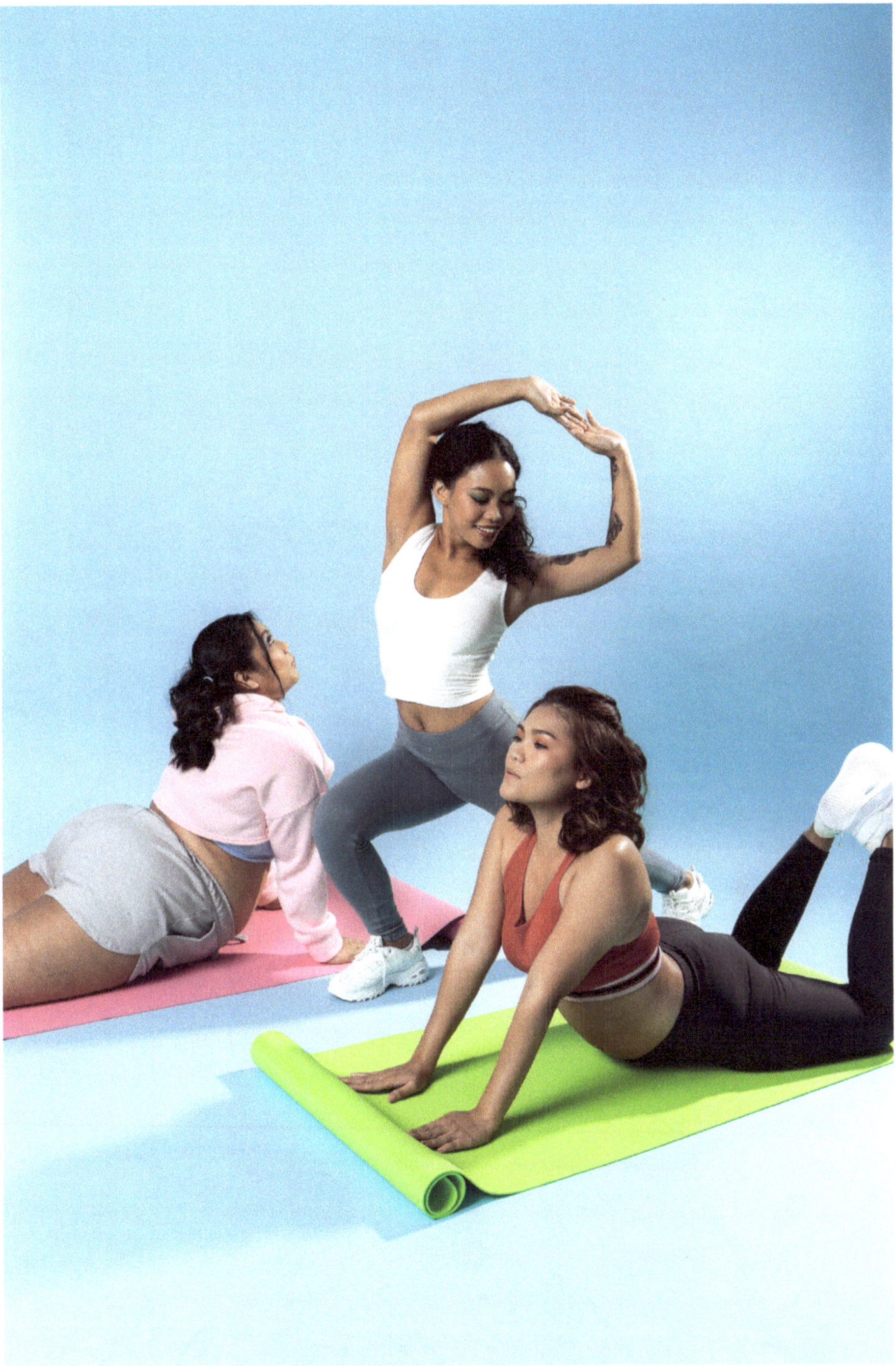

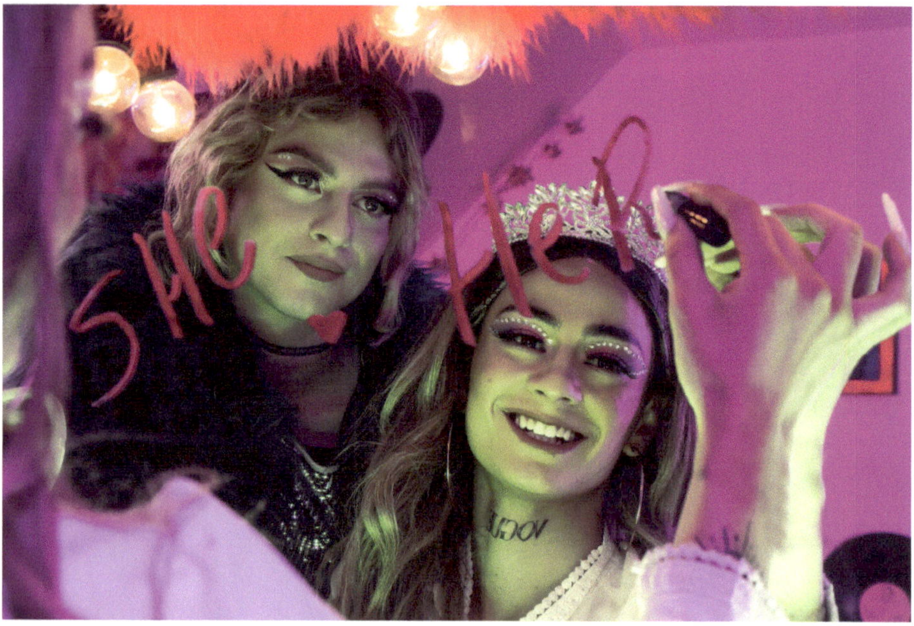
SHE HER

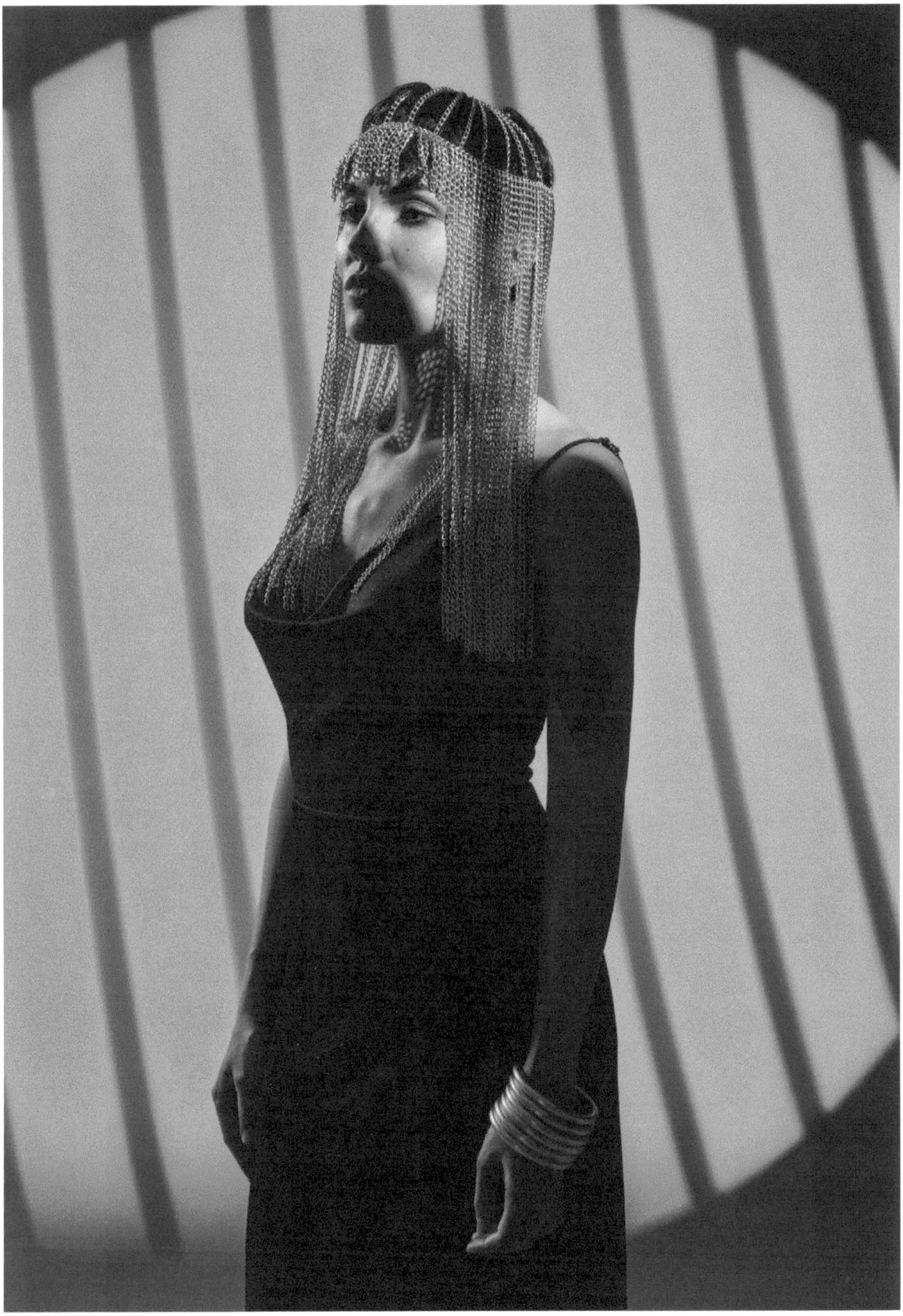

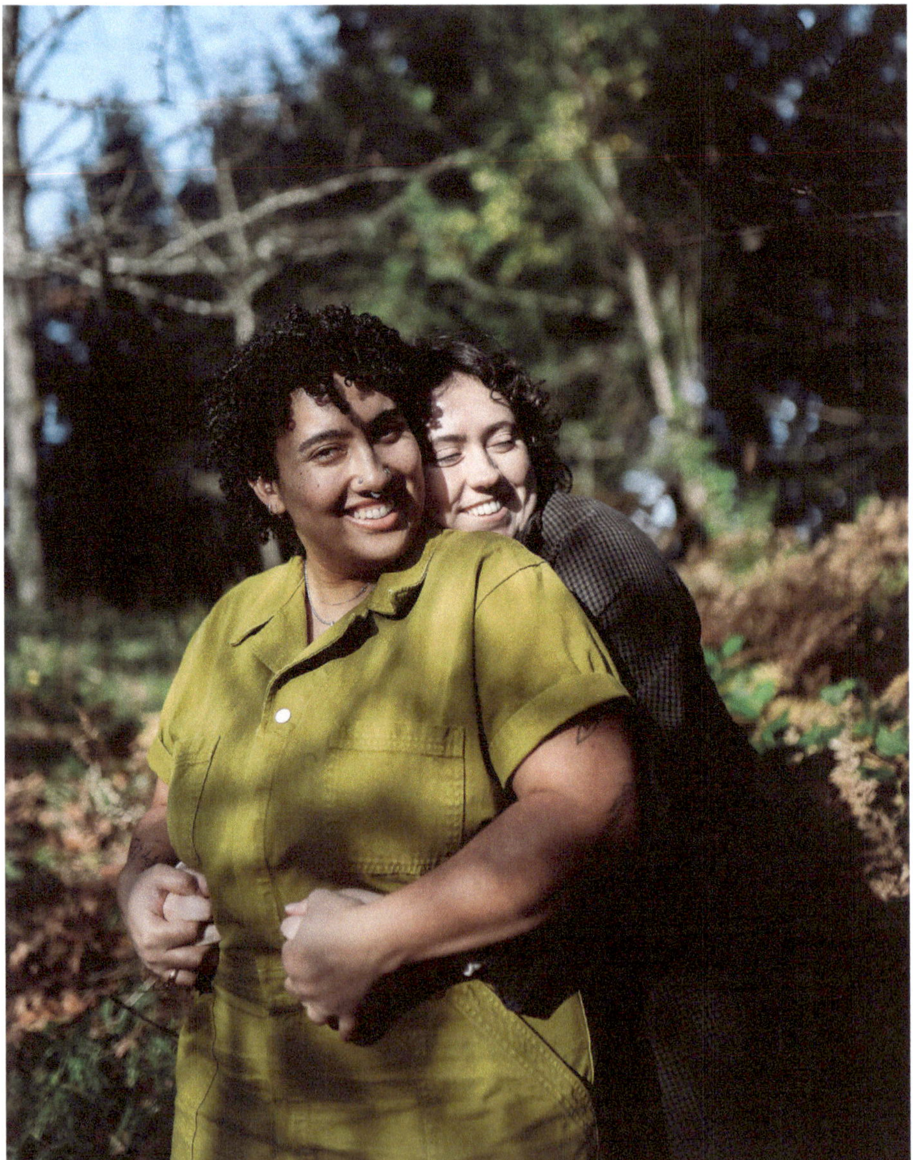

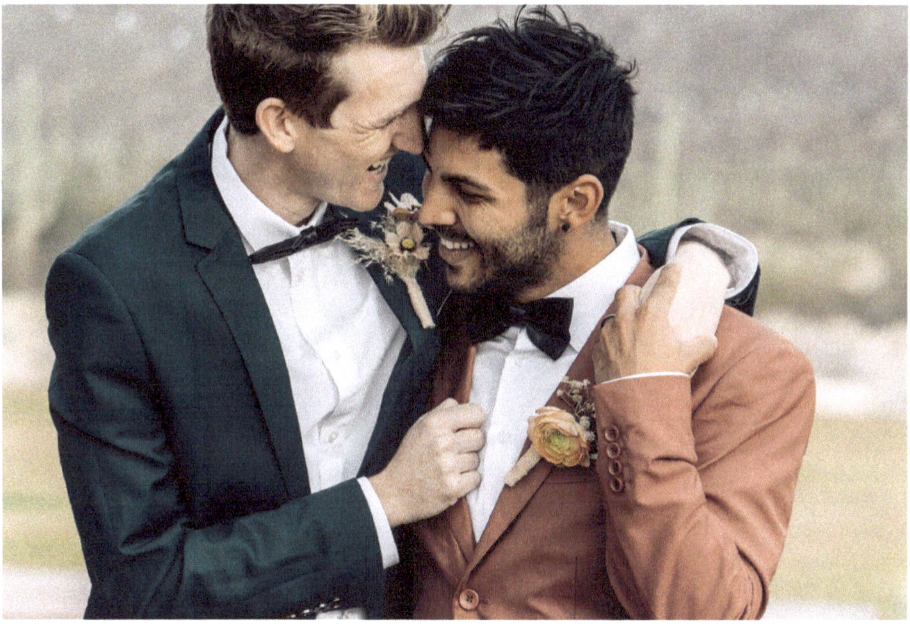

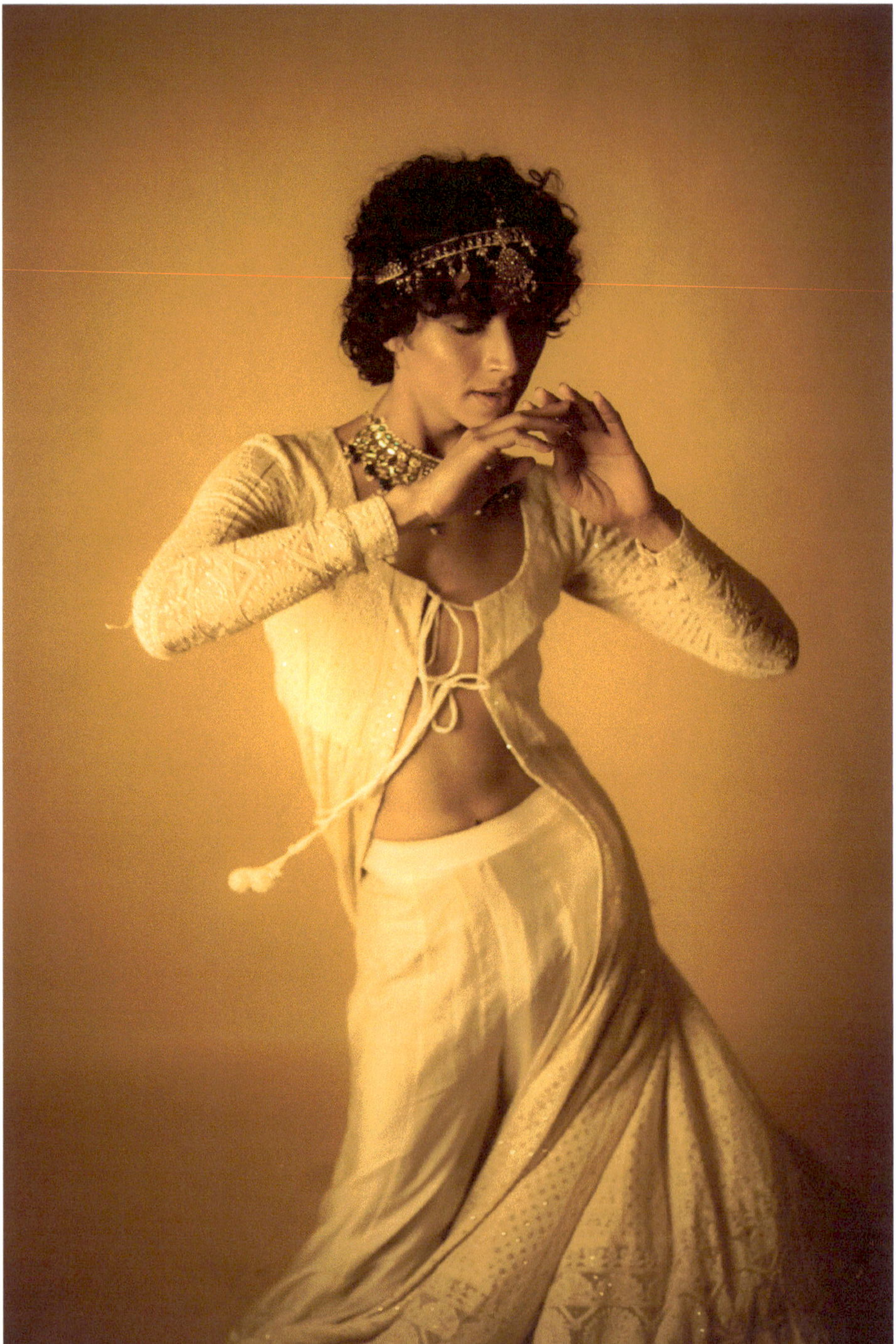

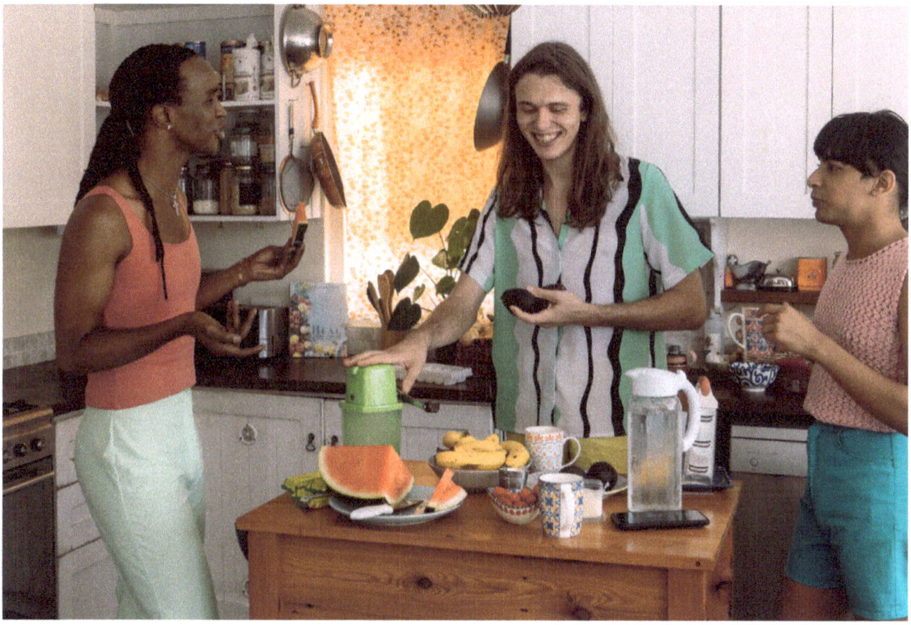

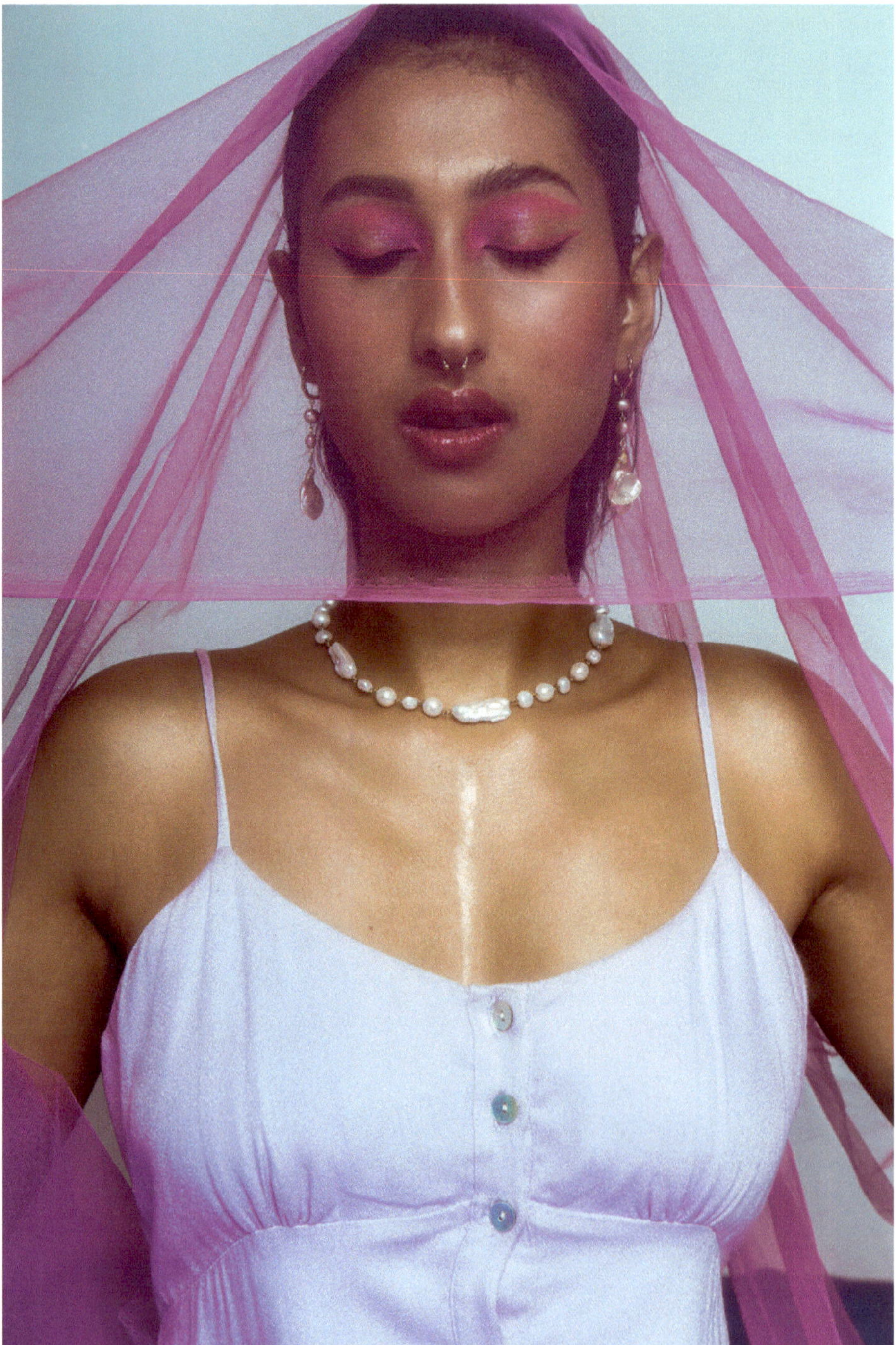

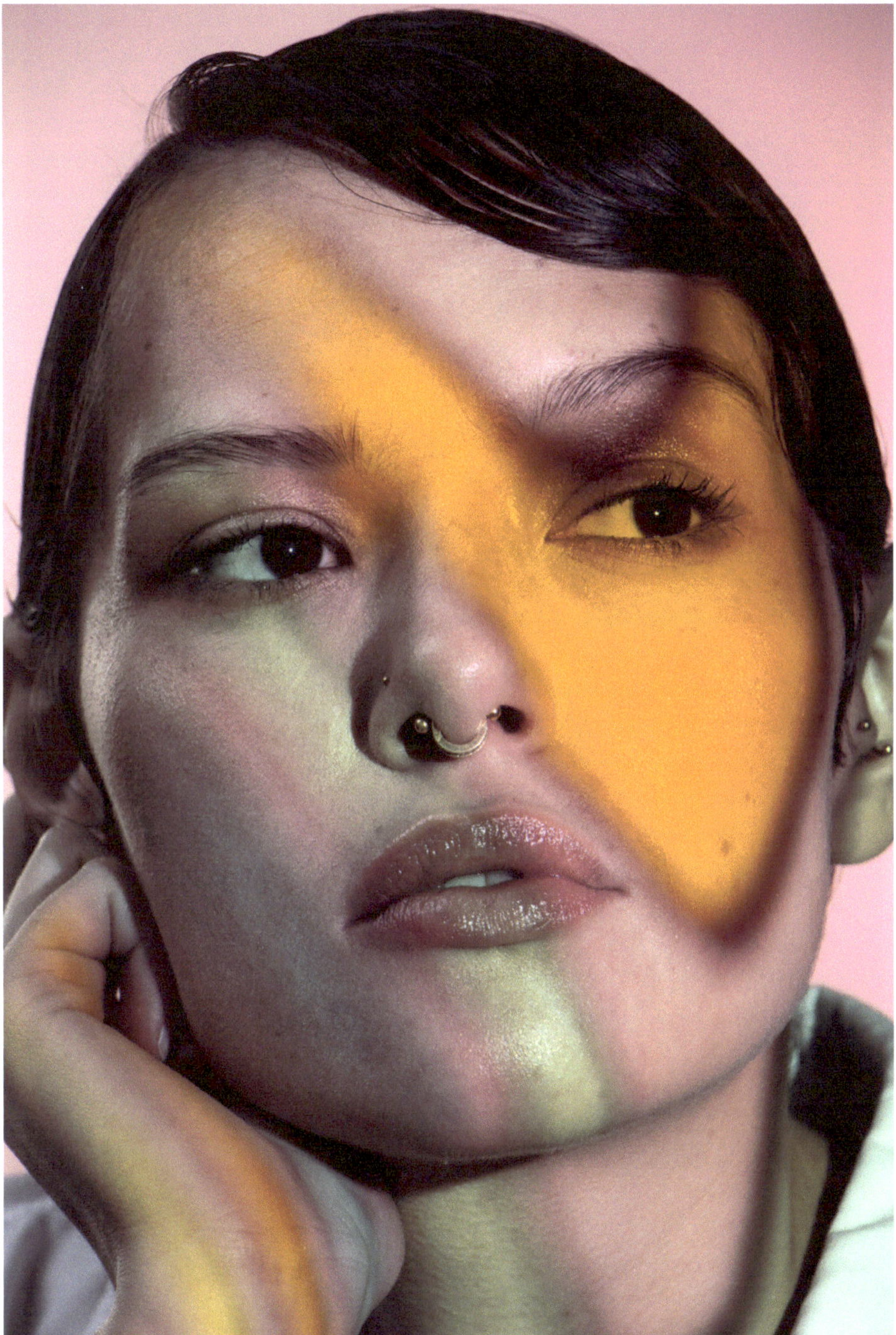

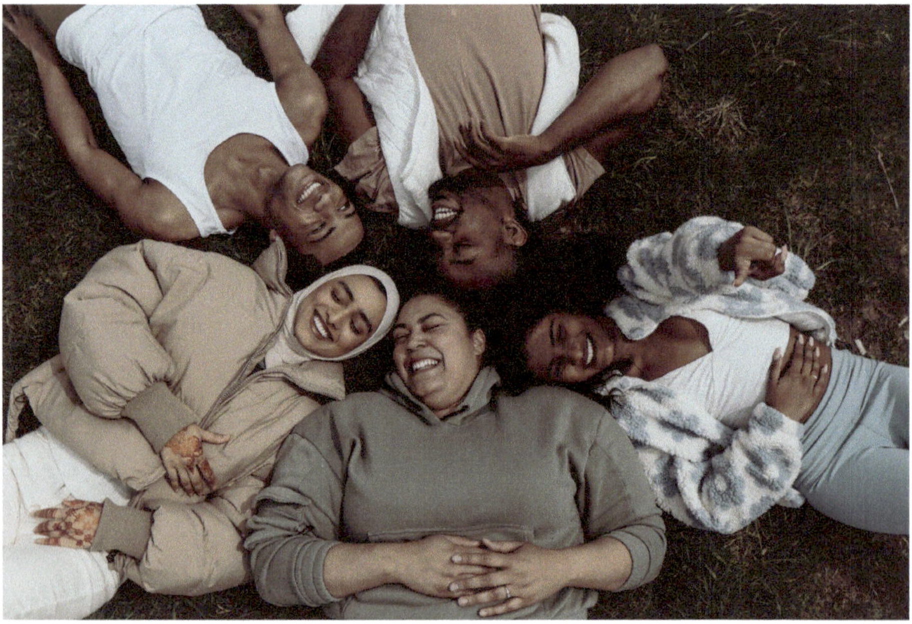

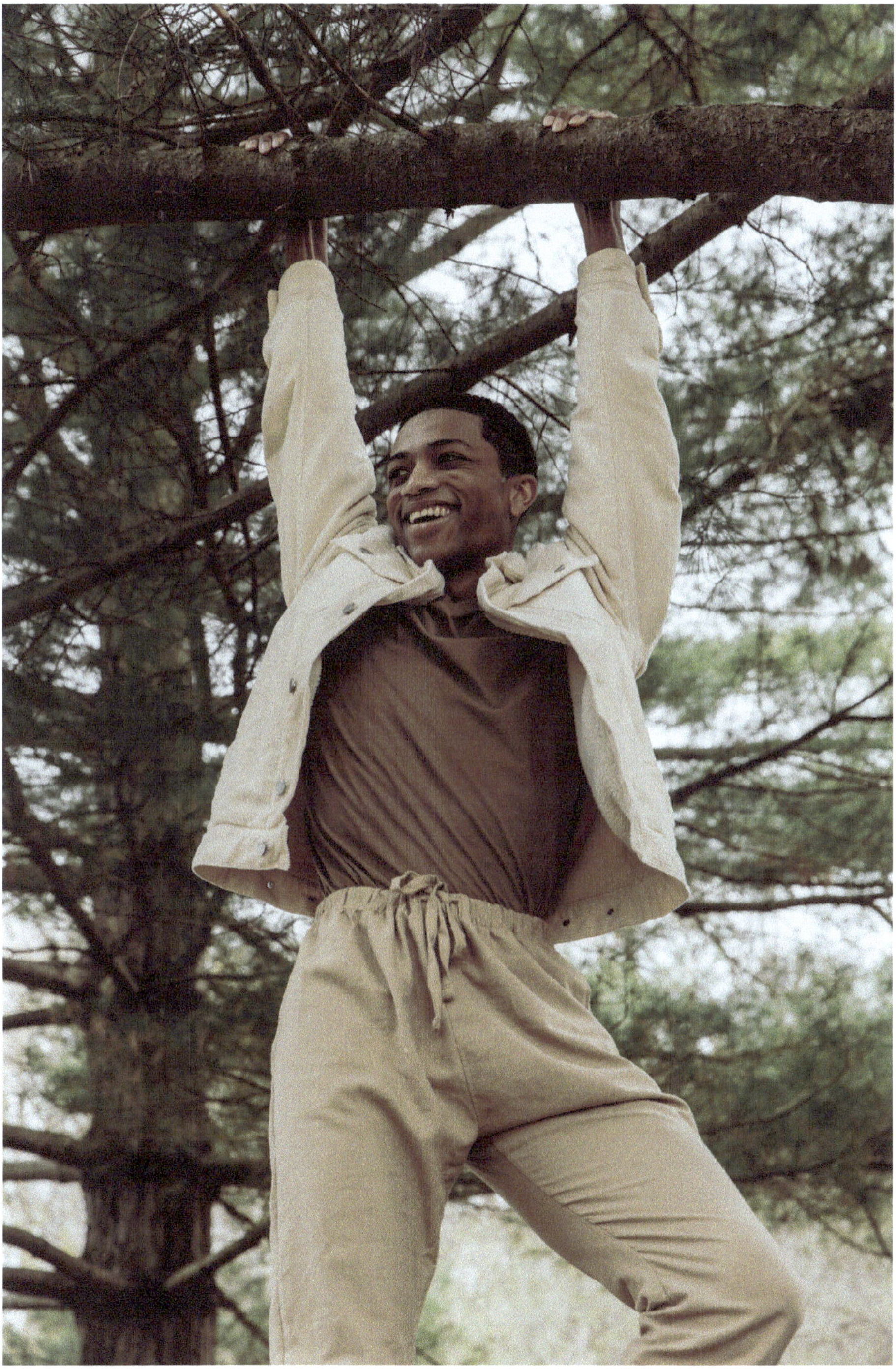

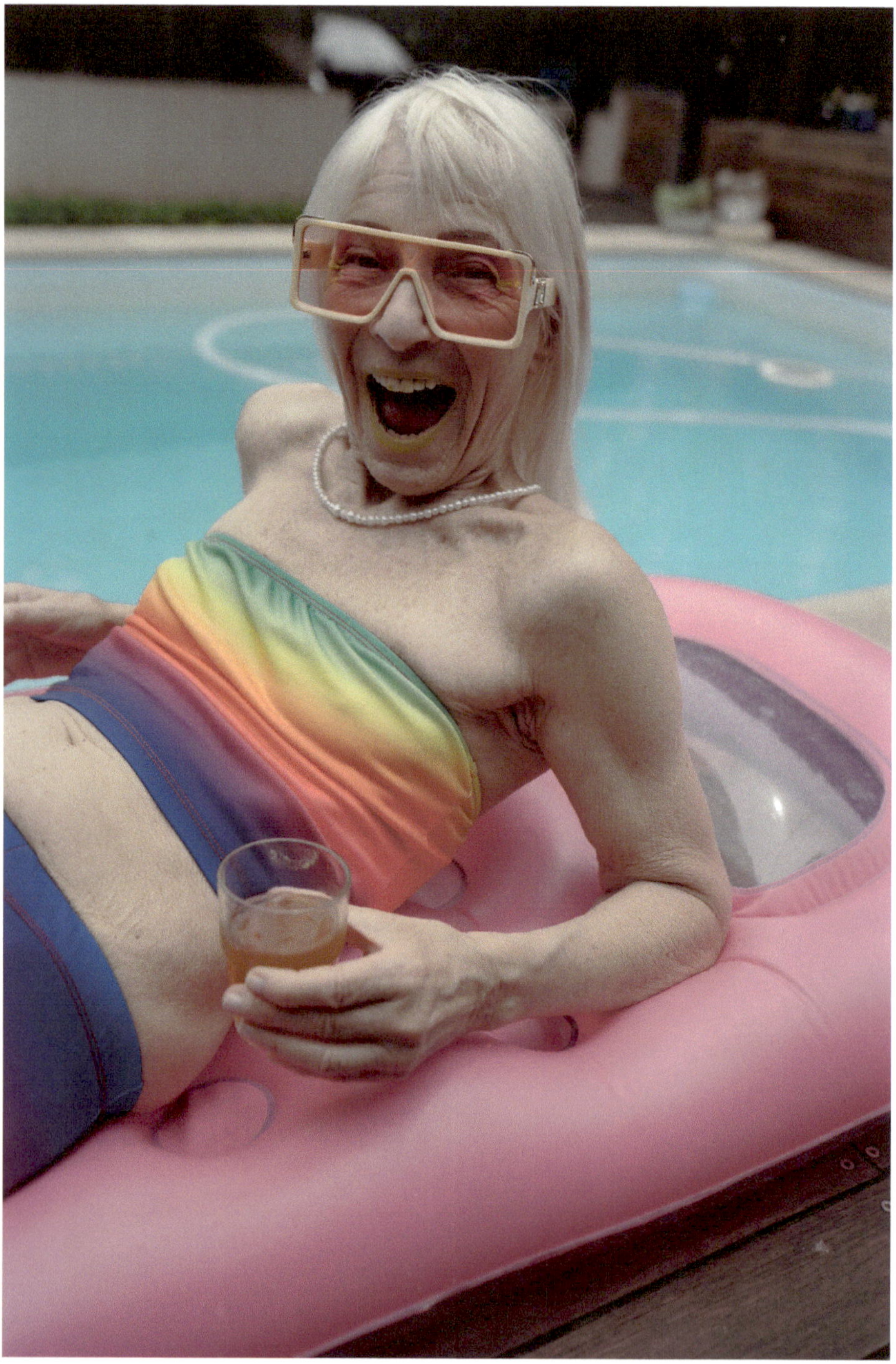

www.ingramcontent.com/pod-product-compliance
Lightning Source LLC
Chambersburg PA
CBHW040334220526
45473CB00009B/2683
* 9 7 9 8 3 6 5 0 1 5 4 0 1 *